Acting in Faith

"For we walk by faith, not by sight"
2 Cor. 5:7

by Philip & Helen Stanley

Adventures in Faith
"For we walk by faith, not by sight"
2 Cor. 5:7

Philip & Helen Stanley
© 2014

All Rights Reserved
ISBN-13: 978-1499562385
ISBN-10: 1499562381

All Scriptures are taken from the New King James unless otherwise stated.

All rights reserved, including the right to reproduce this book, or any portions thereof, in any form. No part of this book may be reproduced or transmitted in any form or by any means without written permission from Philip & Helen Stanley. All rights for publishing this book or portions thereof in other languages are contracted by the author.

Many thanks to Jim and Laura Davis for their patient professional help in the graphic design, editing and publishing of this book. I'm not sure what we would have done without their efficient and timely help. They were a God-send. (They could be reached at jimdavisor.com.)

Dedication

We would like to dedicate this book to our three children who have without complaint gone through many of these experiences with us. Thank you Jon, Sarah and Rachel for the many times that you have stood behind us and prayed for us throughout the years.

Jon, Sarah & Rachel

It would be impossible to express our appreciation to all who have influenced our lives in so many different ways by your fellowship, giving, prayers, teaching and encouragement; but we want to say a big heartfelt thanks to each of you. Some have already gone before to their eternal reward; we look forward to meeting them again one day.

"For we walk by faith, not by sight"—2 Cor. 5:7

Adventures of Faith

One time I heard a missionary tell about how God had called him to Surinam. He said that one day Jesus was walking by and He said, "I am going to Surinam. Would you like to go with Me?" The man's response was, "Yes."

Like that missionary, we too feel that God has allowed us to go with Him. In this book we would like to tell what it has meant to us to accompany Jesus as He has gone to different parts of the world. What a blessing it has been to walk with Him and to share in some of His experiences.

We have been learning that God is interested in even the smallest details of our lives as we commit ourselves fully to Him. It is truly a faith walk, but He is always there to hold our hands and lift us up if we falter. We pray that God will bless you and enrich your lives, and that some of our experiences will prove helpful to you.

Table of Contents

Dedication 3
Adventures of Faith 4

Early Days

Chapter 1
Small Beginnings 7

Chapter 2
Early Memories 10

Chapter 3
Childhood Milestones 12

Chapter 4
The Burden Is Lifted 15

Chapter 5
The Great Deliverance 17

Growing Up Spiritually

Chapter 6
Called to Serve 19

Chapter 7
Pennsylvania 25

Chapter 8
Following Jesus:
1945 and On 28

Courtship and Married Life

Chapter 9
To Go or Not To Go? 35

Chapter 10
Sweet Bliss 39

Chapter 11
Finally Married! 43

Chapter 12
Ahead of Me! 47

Chapter 13
A Sweet Addition 50

Chapter 14
Can God Provide
for Three, Too? 55

Answering the Call to India

Chapter 15
The Voyage 58

Chapter 16
Duped 63

Chapter 17
Following Jesus 66

Chapter 18
Reunited with
The Jennings 71

Chapter 19
What's It Like to
Be in the Zoo 74

Chapter 20
Hot, Hotter, Hottest 77

"For we walk by faith, not by sight"—2 Cor. 5:7 • 5

Winding Roads to Mexico

Chapter 21
Homeward Bound 79

Chapter 22
What Did You Say, God? 83

Chapter 23
More Lessons Learned Off the Beaten Path 85

Chapter 24
Mexico 88

The God of Supply

Chapter 25
The Unplanned Stop 94

Chapter 26
The Land of Leis 100

Chapter 27
Waco or Bust! 106

Chapter 28
God Provides Again 108

The Next Thirty Years

Chapter 29
Adventures in L.A. 1963–1968 113

Chapter 30
Life in Japan 118

Chapter 31
Is She Dying? 124

Chapter 32
Back to Japan 126

Chapter 33
Is This the Right Place? 129

Chapter 34
The Flood 133

Chapter 35
Birth of Miyoshi Bible Church 138

Overcoming Challenges in Faith

Chapter 36
As Birds Flying: 1983 145

Chapter 37
God Answers a Big Request 147

Chapter 38
There's That Old Mosquito! 152

Chapter 39
The Deep, Dark Trial 154

Chapter 40
What Did 'Like Caleb' Mean? 156

Chapter 41
Meeting Pastor Onesimus 159

Chapter 42
Mexico, Here We Come! 165

In Closing
To The Regions Beyond 167

Chapter 1

Small Beginnings
—Helen—

During a church service in India in a hot, windowless room, an Indian lady leaned over to me and whispered, "They're waiting outside to stone you." Looking in my lap at our precious son who was only a little over a year old, I wondered, "What will happen if a stone hits him?" As we have followed the Lord to the lands of our calling, we have often been confronted by various challenges. A major challenge occurred even during each of our childhoods. I'll tell you about mine.

My father was just trying to find his place in the construction business, and he had to be out of town a lot; thus, it was no surprise that he happened to be away when mother went into labor before my birth. Speeding down the highway at seventy miles an hour, Dad was trying his best to reach the hospital in Abilene, Texas before I made my appearance that dark night of Sept. 14, 1932; but he was greatly hindered by having to fix five flat tires along the way. Mother, who had spent several months in bed while she was carrying me, was being brought to Abilene in an ambulance from the small town of Winters, Texas, over thirty miles away. It was almost a miracle that I was actually born in a hospital since even the ambulance had to stop three times to fix a flat!

Dad had planned to name me James Hamilton, so my nickname could be one of his favorite foods—Ham and Eggs; however I turned out to be a girl, so mother named me Helen after her beloved deceased sister.

"For we walk by faith, not by sight"—2 Cor. 5:7 • **7**

While Mother was carrying me, she needed to spend some months in bed. During that time, she had a vivid vision of Christ on the cross, which greatly affected her life. When I was about one year old, I had several sicknesses one after the other. Finally one night it appeared that I was dying. Once again Daddy was out on a job and Mother was alone with my older sister Marian and me. She put her hand on the telephone to call the doctor, but God spoke to her in an audible voice saying, "If you call the doctor, she will be dead by the time he gets here." Having a holy fear of God, she put the phone down, placed a wet cloth on my forehead, made me as comfortable as possible, and went into the adjoining room to pray. She even closed the door behind her. During that long, lonely night she would check on me from time to time while she earnestly pleaded for my life. As she told me many times later, it was her sincere desire to make a vow to God to raise me to serve Him. But knowing her own human weakness, she was afraid she would not be able to fulfill this vow, so she didn't make it. In the morning my fever broke; then she called the doctor. As the doctor listened to mother's description of what had happened during the night, he replied, "I can tell that she has just passed through a crisis." God had spared my life.

In those days of the Great Depression, my family knew what it was to be poor. Mother wore cardboard in her shoes to keep her feet from touching the ground and my only sister Marian, who was just starting school, had to wait for some time before our family could afford to spend five cents for the crayons she needed. But Dad was a hard worker, having begun his construction business by digging holes for fence posts. During his childhood he hardly had a change of clothes. As the youngest among seven brothers and sisters, there weren't a lot of clothes or food to go around. His mother died while he was still a baby and he was raised by his father's second wife whom he affectionately referred to as Auntie. (She, too, died before I was born.) Dad contracted tuberculosis, so he ended up with one kidney and a fused spine. He and mother met in the sanatorium where he was a patient and she was a nurse who had recovered from tuberculosis. At the time of their wedding, Dad had only been given one year to live, so some people were in tears during the ceremony. Mother prayed constantly for him and he lived to the age of eighty-seven, having outlived every member of his family. By the time I came along, our family finances were better.

Even though Mother had not made a vow when I was dying, she did not forget God; her hunger continued to increase. When I was five years old, Mother began reading the Bible every evening. When I saw her with her Bible, I would go up to her and ask her to read it to me, but she would answer, "You can't understand it." My answer was always, "Yes, I can." Eventually she tenderly lifted me into her lap. Thus began a wonderful time of studying God's Word together. If there is one thing that I appreciate the most about my mother, it is the fact that she taught me God's Word; she showed me the way to eternal life by instilling a love for God in my heart. Throughout the years she faithfully read the Bible to me and prayed with me every night. We would memorize scriptures together, and as I grew older, we would teach each other. Many times we would make a game out of our memory work and Bible study. This continued until the day I was married.

Speaking of marriage, God was working on that even before I was born, for a precious little boy was born to Thomas Harvey Stanley and Jean Louise Stanley in South Bend, Indiana on January 25, 1927. He was the only child of his traveling evangelist parents. While Harvey and Louise were ministering in Mississippi, their baby son Philip contracted malaria, compounded by double pneumonia. Even though it got to the point that the doctor said nothing more could be done to save Philip's life, the prayers of his believing parents and other Christians brought him through. Amazingly, both Philip and I both almost died while we were only one! Now in 2014 Philip has reached the ripe age of eighty-seven, and I am less than six years behind him.

Chapter 2

Early Memories

—Philip—

Belief in healing actually began before my parents were ever married. It all began with my mother when she was twenty years old. At that time she was almost blind and had to wear thick glasses. Mother came in contact with the gospel at Cadle Tabernacle in Indianapolis, Indiana. F.F. Bosworth, a well-known evangelist, was preaching salvation and healing. In the meetings she came to know Christ as her Savior, and she had prayer for her eyes. Nothing happened at the time, but two days later something snapped in her head and she was completely healed. She didn't need her glasses anymore, not even to read. Mother went to be with the Lord when she was ninety-four, and she still didn't wear glasses. She could read well, hear well, and she wasn't taking any medications.

Mother and Father married not long after her salvation and healing. Father worked for Studebaker Car Company in South Bend, Indiana, but upon receiving a call from God to be an evangelist, he didn't let any grass grow under his feet. I barely had time to be born before my parents started traveling to hold gospel meetings. Father was a minister of the gospel for forty of the sixty-two years of his life. He pastored Nazarene churches and a Methodist church, but the best years of his ministry were the last twenty in which he ministered as an evangelist.

During the Depression, Father preached anywhere he could. Later when we were in Boone, Iowa, he began working for the railroad. This kept us from starving. As a child I knew deep poverty. This continued until I was twenty-five years old, but praise the Lord, there was a bright side to those days of poverty! One Sunday night when my father was preaching, I understood my need of a Savior. As I knelt on the gravel floor of Gospel Tabernacle weeping real tears of repentance, I asked God to save me. Afterward I felt so light and free. I was just seven years old, but I will never forget that life-changing experience which has lasted from then until now.

I have never backslidden or desired to turn to the world. That doesn't mean that I was always perfect. One time when my parents told me not to go to the movies, I slipped off and went anyway. When my father found out about it, he gave me a spanking that I have never forgotten. That was the last time I ever sneaked off to the movies. One more time a blistering spanking brought deliverance to me—when I had stolen some of the church money that was kept in a jar in the church and my parents found out about it!

"For we walk by faith, not by sight"—2 Cor. 5:7

Chapter 3

Childhood Milestones

—Helen—

My childhood was a happy one as we moved from place to place in Texas, Oklahoma and New Mexico, following Dad and his construction business. One unforgettable experience took place while we were living in Boise City, Oklahoma in 1935. I was just three years old. We started to drive to our friends' house about thirty miles away, as Dad was going to meet us there and we were all going to eat together. Since moving to Boise City, we had heard stories about the terrible black dust

Helen (L) with her sister Marian

storms that sometimes blew in unexpectedly. People had said you couldn't even see your hand in front of your face during a storm, but you know how people can exaggerate! "That couldn't be true," we thought.

On that particular day as we stopped at a gas station, we looked at the sky and saw a huge black cloud moving along the ground not far away. What should we do? Mother decided that we should head back home, but we had only gone a short distance when the storm overtook us. I remember screaming, "I can't breathe," while Mother strained to see if she could catch a glimpse of the edge of the road enough to find her way. Barely inching, we finally arrived home. Mother and Marian held me tightly to keep me from blowing away in the strong wind as we made our way from the car to the house. That experience made believers out of us—we hadn't been able to see our own hands in front of our faces!

I was about ten when I went to a Christian summer camp. I was having quite a good time—until the next-to-the-last day. That night there was to be a camp fire. Each one at the camp was to take a little block of wood in their hand, give their testimony, and then cast the wood into the fire. That whole afternoon I was sitting on my bed trying to figure out what I could say. As I was there with my paper and a pencil in my hand, another girl came by and asked me if I was a Christian. How well I remember the battle that went on in my mind. I was thinking, "I have gone to Sunday School and to church every Sunday as long as I can remember. I read the Bible. Everyone thinks I am a Christian, but I have no assurance in my heart. I can't say that I am not a Christian; that would be embarrassing." Finally, I answered, "Yes," but I was only left with doubts in my heart. I don't even remember what I did or didn't say that night, but I have never forgotten my intense struggle that afternoon.

When I was twelve I decided to join the church and be sprinkled on Easter Sunday. I really looked forward to a change, but afterwards I felt so empty and disappointed. Nothing had happened to me. I still felt the same. On the front of the church bulletin that Sunday was a pretty picture of the cross and Easter lilies. Mother had the picture framed so that I could remember the occasion, but every time I looked at it, I would only be reminded of my disappointment and emptiness.

One day when I was in the fifth grade we heard the awful news at school that Pearl Harbor had been bombed. We were at war with

Japan. Young men started going off to war. Ration books were issued for shoes, coffee, butter, sugar and gasoline. Since nylons were unavailable, you could buy liquid with which you could "paint" your nylons on your legs, complete with a painted seam that was supposed to go straight up the back of your leg. (Seamless hose didn't yet exist.) I remember going out with a friend after school to collect used bacon grease and lard from neighbors, so that it could be used to help in the war effort. Some of my relatives were drafted into the service. Things were different in America; everything and everyone was focused on the war effort.

My mother's brother was among those who were called. Uncle John ended up in California for a time before being sent overseas, and my aunt went to California with him. While they were there, Aunt Clara went to a Foursquare church service and was saved and filled with the Holy Spirit. Her life and lifestyle completely changed. She had been a snuff-dipping hillbilly before, and now she was a happy, born-again Christian. When she and Uncle John visited us sometime later, they told us about the Baptism in the Holy Spirit and took us to a church in Dallas, Texas where we were then living. It was a little wooden church with a wooden floor, and I didn't understand what was happening. Some ladies were dancing, and it made the whole building shake. Other people were shouting. To cap it all, a group of people gathered around someone at the end of the service and started praying for that individual. I couldn't figure out what they were doing to the person. It all sounded and looked so strange that after the service I said, "I will never go to a service like that again . . . unless God tells me to." I really didn't expect that God would ever tell me to either!

I was totally against the whole thing, but Mother's spiritual appetite was just whetted by what she had seen and heard, so she began visiting services from time to time. Finally, she got so hungry for God that she made the decision that she was going to go and pray for the Holy Spirit, whether I ever went with her or not. By this time my sister was away in college, and my dad had never been much of a church-goer, so I was the only one that Mother had any real spiritual fellowship with in our family. It was a real sacrifice for her to make the decision to go alone, but God saw her heart, and He was about to give her an answer.

Chapter 4

The Burden Is Lifted

—Helen—

In 1944, World War II was still in progress. The Christian Servicemen's Center in downtown Dallas was a place where servicemen could go to relax and have some refreshments. They would be served by Christian volunteers. On this particular day, Mother decided to volunteer at the center, so I went to meet her there after school. As it so happened, only one other person was there the rest of the day, and that person was a young Bible school student from a town about thirty miles away. As the student and Mother discussed the Word of God together, I silently listened to them talk about the Baptism of the Holy Spirit and other spiritual truths. When the day ended and it was time to go home, I felt different. The servicemen's center was upstairs in a building. Walking down the stairs and out into the open, it was as if someone had lifted a heavy load off of my back. The birds seemed to sing sweeter and the grass appeared to be greener. Everything felt wonderful. As I looked back on that day sometime after, I realized that was the day when I had opened my heart to the Word of God that I had been hearing all of my life. I had not knelt down and prayed a sinner's prayer; I had just believed and received God's forgiveness for my sins. I had been born again and become God's child. The emptiness and searching that I had felt in my heart had been filled . . . never to be empty again. The peace of God had filled my life. I was thirteen years old. What did God have in store for me now?

The first thing I said to Mother after being born again was, "I will go with you to a Spirit-filled service now." You can imagine the rejoicing in Mother's heart, for this was just after she had made the decision to follow on with God, whether I went with her or not; she had not yet had the opportunity to attend another service, so she never had to go alone after she made her consecration to God.

Soon we had the opportunity to attend a revival meeting. The evangelist was a fiery preacher named Jack Coe, and I still remember the subject of his message. He preached out of the book of Exodus about the mixed multitude of people who came out of Egypt, and how they were always complaining. The service was strange and noisy, just like the first service I had attended earlier. Some people were dancing and many were speaking in tongues. In fact, I remember thinking, "This just sounds like a lot of cattle making noise." This time however, my reaction was different from the first time. I got down on my knees and prayed, "Lord, I don't understand this, but please help me to understand." And He did. From that day on, I became hungry for more of God; I wanted to be filled with the Holy Spirit.

Of course, all this about the Holy Spirit was still new to me. Now whenever I would read my Bible, it seemed that there were references to the Holy Spirit every place I read. The Bible was full of such verses! I still had questions. One was, "Why would we have to speak in tongues?" I was pointed to James 3:7–8. *"For every kind of beast and bird, of reptile and creature of the sea, is tamed and has been tamed by mankind. But no man can tame the tongue. It is an unruly evil, full of deadly poison."* My tongue really needed taming, and God was about to do it.

This began a period of time when Mother and I began earnestly seeking God for the baptism in the Holy Spirit. We would go to those services every chance we had, while still being faithful to attend the church in which we were members. We would stay after each service to pray on our knees at the altar in the front of the church. How I loved the altars! I still miss them today in churches, for the altars were a place where we could go and pour out our heart to God. It was a time when the message which had just been preached could take further root in our hearts. The altar is a place where we can have fellowship with God and leave our burdens. *"Even the sparrow has found a home, And the swallow a nest for herself, Where she may lay her young—Even Your altars, O Lord of hosts, My King and my God.(Ps. 84:3)."* God gave me many blessings as I sought Him, and one afternoon about six months later I finally spoke in tongues.

Chapter 5

The Great Deliverance

—Helen—

Even though I was only thirteen, I would go to the ladies' meetings every chance I got. I loved to hear the advice the ladies would give each other about how to be successful Christians and obedient wives, plus it was another opportunity to pray for the Holy Spirit Baptism. One particular Thursday afternoon, the ladies spent several hours praying with me. The next morning Mother, Marian and I were scheduled to visit some of our relatives in another city, and I wanted to be filled before I went. As I sat in a

The day after receiving the Baptism in the Holy Spirit

church pew with different ones praying for me, I began speaking in stammering lips as in Is. 28:11-12. The ladies encouraged me to just keep speaking, even though it sounded strange—more like babies' gibberish when they make their first sounds. As I continued speaking, I was instructed to just yield my tongue and lips completely to God. I realized that being filled with the Spirit is something like learning to float in the water. We just surrender everything to God, and He begins to speak through us in a new language. Oh, what joy it is to hear ourselves praising and worshipping God in a language we have never learned! The Spirit prays through us and refreshes us when we yield to Him.

Mother rejoiced that I had been filled with the Spirit, but she was disappointed that she hadn't received, too. We went home from church and prepared for our next day's journey. It was late before Mother was finally ready to crawl into bed. It had been her custom during the preceding months to spend some time asking God for the Holy Spirit each night before going to bed, but this night she was just too tired. However, at the last moment she decided that she would just lie down on the floor by her bed and thank God for a few minutes before retiring. As she did this, the power of God came down and mightily filled her. In her words she said, "Waves of God's love swept into me beginning at my toes and fingertips, and each wave landed in my heart. This continued until I felt that I could contain no more. I felt as though I was just one big heart!" She began speaking in tongues and glorifying God in a loud voice. We happily left the next morning on our trip.

There was one thing the church ladies had carefully instructed me to do; ever since then I have been exceedingly grateful for their advice. They told me that I should speak in tongues every day. We left home the day after I was filled, but I found that after we arrived at our relatives' house, I could no longer speak in tongues. Remembering the instructions the ladies had given me the day before, I went out to the garage, closed the door, and stayed until I could once again pray in tongues. This has been a great help to me, for I have had continual liberty from that time until this. We have prayed with many people through the years who have once had the experience of being filled and speaking in tongues, but they did not continue on. They had no liberty and were not enjoying the benefits until they were prayed for once again.

Being filled with the Spirit brought me many blessings. God's Word was like a new book, for John 14:15–26 says that Jesus will send us a Comforter, a Helper, Who will live in us and teach us. He will reveal more of Christ to us.

As for the taming of my tongue, God had an added surprise for me. My parents used to tell me that I never cried like a normal baby—I screamed! I had temper-tantrums! One day when I was at school just a few days after being filled with the Spirit, I suddenly realized that there was something different about me. I wasn't losing my temper as I had before. The Lord had delivered me from the root of anger that had been plaguing me, and what a deliverance it was!

Chapter 6

Called to Serve

—Philip—

When I was fourteen my mother and father separated, never to come together again. They were never divorced, nor did either one ever remarry. I stayed with my mother, and at the age of sixteen it was necessary for me to begin working to support my mother and me. It surely wasn't easy, but I leaned on the Lord and He helped me. During this time,

Philip and his mother

I became more devoted to the Lord. God gave me a good friend named James Parker when I attended the First Baptist Church in San Jose, California. James and I would go and pass out tracts on the street on weekends, and I would do that at my job, too. I learned to be a personal witness. On Sunday evenings before church, we would go out into the street and invite people to the Sunday evening service. The church always had an altar call for salvation, so I would pray with those who came for prayer.

During the years of World War II, my mother and I were praying I wouldn't have to go to war. When I turned eighteen, I had to register for the draft. I took a physical and passed with a 1-A classification; however, for some reason they stamped on my papers to come back in six months. At that time we were living in California, but we decided to move to Montana. By the time my draft papers were transferred, the war was over. It was then that something strange happened—I

"For we walk by faith, not by sight"—2 Cor. 5:7

received a letter from the government telling me that I had to report to be inducted. Really, I couldn't understand why this would happen after God had so wonderfully delivered me from going during the war, but God definitely had His reasons, which I was soon to find out. When induction time came, I was given the choice of entering either the Army Air Force or the Navy. I chose the Army Air Force. Immediately I was sent to Shepherd Field in Wichita Falls, Texas, where I went through basic training. I hated it so much that I said to myself, "I'll never go back to Texas again!" (Be careful what you say lest you have to eat your own words.)

After basic training I was sent to California for six months. It was there that God let me meet a Christian soldier who had an interest in the Holy Spirit. Even though he said he didn't believe in speaking in tongues, he was attending some Pentecostal services, so I went with him a few times.

Salt Lake City

Just before shipping out to Japan, I was sent to Salt Lake City for three weeks. There I found an Assembly of God church near the base. Because it was a much persecuted church, the people were extra spiritual. Some believers were losing their jobs and others were having serious things happen to them because of their stand for Christ. There was prayer at the altar before and after each service, and the people would freely pray in tongues. Even though I didn't believe in the tongues, hearing them speak didn't seem to bother me.

During one Sunday morning service, I was greatly blessed. We sang "This World Is Not My Home" and "His Face Will Outshine Them All". This made me think of the glorious hope we have in Christ, and about how Jesus Christ's face will outshine all others when we get to Heaven. I was blessed like I had never been blessed before. I praised God and felt like shouting. By the time we got to the second song, I felt like I had already gone to Heaven. It was an experience that helped prepare me to later be filled with the Holy Spirit. I submitted a request to be able to stay in Salt Lake City, but the Army Air Force and God had other plans for me.

Japan

The time to be shipped overseas came, and I was sent to the 5th Air Force Headquarters in Tokyo, Japan. My harsh military life suddenly and drastically changed, for I was stationed in a building right in the center of downtown Tokyo, where we lived very high for army life. Our evening meals were served at tables set in real style. We were even serenaded by an orchestra or treated with some other kind of entertainment while we ate.

One day I looked on the bulletin board and saw an announcement that said the GI Gospel Hour would meet on Saturday nights at the Ginza Methodist Church. That really interested me, so I attended the next Saturday. Before the service was to start, they had a prayer meeting on the roof. As I heard the men praying, I noticed that one of them was speaking in other tongues. I thought, "I want to get acquainted with that man," and so I did. His name was Robert Posey. My life was about to change.

"For we walk by faith, not by sight"—2 Cor. 5:7

Rooftop Experience ~ 1946

Those were wonderful days right after the war in 1946. General MacArthur requested that the churches in America send 3,000 missionaries to evangelize Japan, but very few came. It was a time when you could preach the gospel anywhere. One of the Japanese pastors with whom I worked had a big drum he would beat loudly while he marched through the street each Sunday afternoon. At the sound of the drum, the children would follow him to his home, where he would have a children's service for them.

Illustration by Junko Suzuki

One day as I was on my cot reading the Bible, God spoke to me and said, "You have not been filled with the Holy Spirit; when you are filled, you will speak in other tongues." This was a real revelation to me, for previously my friend had twice asked me in a very nice way if I was filled with the Spirit and I had answered, "Yes." He then had asked me if I had spoken in other tongues, but I had replied that I didn't think that was necessary. Now God had changed my mind, and I was eager to be filled. Two nights later when I saw my friend Robert at a home meeting, I told him what God had spoken to me. He said, "Why don't you come to my building and spend the night with me tonight?" So it was that about 11:00 pm that same night, we went up on the roof to pray for the infilling of the Holy Spirit. In about thirty minutes I began to be filled and speak in other tongues. It was such a glorious experience that when later I tried to go down and catch some sleep, I couldn't stay in bed, so I just returned to the rooftop and continued to enjoy the Holy Spirit some more. I have been speaking in tongues ever since! Truly, I have daily been edified, as 1 Cor. 14:4 says, *"He that who speaks in a tongue edifies himself."* Daily I have received a fresh filling of the Holy Spirit. What a wonderful change there has been in my life! One difference I noticed immediately was that I liked to pray by the hour; also, I received more

Chiyoe Nizuka

power to become a witness.

An amazing thing was that General MacArthur allowed the army vehicles to be used to preach the gospel. Robert and I took advantage of this and would go out to preach, but I needed an interpreter. In answer to prayer the Lord provided a young Japanese girl to be my interpreter. Fortunately, I didn't fall in love with her! I did share with her about being filled with the Holy Spirit. A few days later she came and said that she had found a church that believed in the Holy Spirit baptism. She had gone there, received prayer and been filled!

The Call

Three months later, I attended a Sunday night service where a medical doctor was speaking about the need for laborers. After the message he gave an invitation for us to present ourselves to the Lord for Him to use. Many of the two hundred soldiers attending were weeping, including me. As I stood there before the Lord with an open heart, God spoke to me and said that He wanted me to go to the world and tell those who had never heard. Soon after this call of God, the U.S. Congress passed a special bill to release a group of us from the military so we could go home, for we were no longer needed. I had only been in the service about sixteen months.

While returning home on the troop ship, God gave me a vivid dream. I was standing in a Japanese train station and people were getting on the train from both sides of the platform. As I stood there, a man who looked like

Illustration by Junko Suzuki

he was made of greenish-gray stone came down the stairway. When he began hitting and hurting the people, they began looking to me to help them. Upon seeing the people looking to me for deliverance, the stone man turned and gave me a solid sock in the jaw. You can imagine how painful it felt, even in my dream, but I turned to the man and said, "I rebuke you in the name of Jesus." Immediately, he was gone!

I have found that when God gives a dream or vision, He is faithful to give the interpretation. This was the interpretation of the dream. The greenish-gray stone man was the idolatry of Japan. (There are many stone idols throughout Japan.) The idolatry was hurting the people, and the people were looking to me to bring deliverance to them. This deliverance would come through the name of Jesus.

After being filled with the Holy Spirit, called to the ministry, and having a vivid dream about the Japanese people, I was ready to return to Japan immediately, but God had another plan. It wasn't until twenty-two years later that God released Helen and me to move to Japan.

Chapter 7

Pennsylvania

—Philip—

God didn't send me back to Japan immediately, and the reason soon became clear. I needed some training, so God began to work on it right away. Mother had been living in California while I was in Japan, and it was there that I was released from the military. Shortly after my release Mother and I moved to Pennsylvania, where I began attending an Assembly of God church. Almost immediately I was made a deacon—and the youth leader! As a leader, I was very zealous. We had a youth meeting before the Sunday night service, a prayer meeting on Tuesday nights, and outreach on Friday nights. God really moved and the gifts of the Spirit began to come into operation in my life. My first experience in the gifts was to interpret a message in tongues in a Sunday night service. I felt like I was being lifted into Heaven as I gave the interpretation. We even began to enter into some praise in our youth meetings. This was praise that we didn't have in the regular church services.

About this time God said, "Move to Dallas, Texas." That was the last place I wanted to go! Remember how I had said to myself after going through basic training in Texas, "I'll never go to Texas again?" God gave me grace to obey anyway, but why of all places did He want me to go there?

Texas

Arriving in Texas, I felt like God had more for me, so I began to search for the right church. One day as I was visiting a certain church for the first time, the Spirit of the Lord came upon me and I didn't know what to do. I said, "Lord, what shall I do?" God said, "Prophesy." I opened my mouth and began to prophesy for the first time. After the service one of the men said to me, "We need more of that in this church."

Actually, this was a period of time when the Lord was restoring the gifts of the Spirit to the church. Before this, the gifts of the Spirit in Pentecostal churches had mainly been limited to the gifts of tongues and the interpretation of tongues. The ministry of the apostles and prophets was almost non-existent, but God began sending rain upon His hungry people. Scriptures like Zechariah 10:1, *"Ask the Lord for rain In the time of the latter rain. The Lord will make flashing clouds; He will give them showers of rain, Grass in the field for everyone."* and Joel 2:23, *"Be glad then, you children of Zion, And rejoice in the Lord your God; For He has given you the former rain faithfully, And He will cause the rain to come down for you—The former rain, And the latter rain in the first month."* became like cornerstones to what God was doing. The visitation became known as the Latter Rain. Songs like "Send Down the Rain, Lord; Send Down the Rain, Lord: Send Down the Latter Rain" were sung often as a prayer to God.

In the beginning of 1949 I made a trip to Waco, Texas. A friend had told me he thought all nine gifts of the Spirit were in operation in a small church there. Glenn Ewing, the pastor of Grace Gospel Church, received me with love and told me of a similar church in Dallas. It really turned out to be the right church, and God began to teach me many new and wonderful things when I started attending there. Actually, the Dallas Gospel Center was in the midst of a special outpouring of the Holy Spirit. During this time God taught me about the flow of the gifts of the Spirit and how God wants to use all the members of His church, and not just the pastor. The abundance of praise to the Lord created a great atmosphere for body ministry.*
I learned that there is a rest for the children of God, a rest that causes us to stop our own works and let Him work through us. I really needed that teaching, and it changed my life.

We were taught about the five ministry offices in Eph. 4:11. Being called to fulltime ministry, I knew that I must have one of the five ministry offices, but I didn't know which one. However, I heard that

---

*Body ministry is when different people are led by the Spirit during a service to share something like a testimony, song, prophecy or an exhortation as in Col 3:16: "Let the word of Christ dwell in you richly in all wisdom; teaching and admonishing one another in psalms and hymns and spiritual songs, singing with grace in your hearts to the Lord."

if I would seek the Lord with fasting and prayer, God would confirm my ministry through the laying on of hands and prophecy, as in Acts 13:1–3:

> Now in the church that was at Antioch there were certain prophets and teachers: Barnabas, Simeon who was called Niger, Lucius of Cyrene, Manaen who had been brought up with Herod the tetrarch, and Saul. As they ministered to the Lord and fasted, the Holy Spirit said, "Now separate to Me Barnabas and Saul for the work to which I have called them." Then, having fasted and prayed, and laid hands on them, they sent them away.

As I sought the Lord diligently, the time came for my ministry to be confirmed. God revealed my calling as an evangelist. This surely gave me more confidence in the function of my ministry. It was now the end of 1949.

A Big Surprise

God had another reason for sending me to Texas—he had a wife for me. While still in Pennsylvania, I had gotten quite serious about one sweet Jewish Christian girl in the church; however, one night I had a vivid dream, warning that I was about to marry the wrong girl, and I should give up my wedding plans, for they were not right. That dream really put the fear of God in my heart, and I stopped that relationship immediately. Now that I was attending the Dallas Gospel Center, God began to start putting some of the missing pieces of my life together. One day a girl and her mother came to the church. When I first saw that girl, I felt she was the one I was to marry, but I said nothing about it to her; in fact, I gave her no special attention in any way. I just prayed and waited for one whole year until God really confirmed to me that she was the right one, then I went into immediate action!

Chapter 8

Following Jesus: 1945 and On

—Helen—

The young Bible school student who was talking to my mother the day I was born again explained to us how he happened to be at the servicemen's center the same day we were. He had awakened that morning and asked, "God, what do you want me to do today?" God had answered, "Go to Dallas." He replied, "I don't have any money, so I can't go." God had said again, "Go to Dallas." Wanting to obey God, he had hitchhiked. I am so glad he was obedient. Besides being obedient, he was nice-looking, too, and he answered my letter when I wrote to thank him. Of course, this was very exciting to me, so I wrote again. When he answered the second time, he signed his letter with loving words; the third time I wrote, he answered and signed it, "*Love always.*" Oh, what a sweet sound to my 13-year-old ears; I was hooked, and I dreamed of him day and night! As time passed without hearing anything again, I wondered what I had written in my last letter that caused him not to answer. "What had I said that was wrong?" Sometime later I got my answer—he had gotten married! It was a good lesson for me, and it shows how changeable people can be. But did God have someone special for me?

I had one great desire—to do God's will in my life. Perhaps even from my childhood days there had been two ambitions stirring within my heart. One was to be a nurse, chemist, or something in the medical field; the other was to become a missionary. In the beginning, my desire was all on the medical side. As a child I would operate on grasshoppers (none survived), nurse my stuffed animals, and even dress up in my real nurse's uniform that mother had had made for me. As I grew and matured, I would hold these desires up to the Lord and ask Him for His guidance. I tried to be willing to do whatever God had for me, but the missionary desire began to increase while the medical desires decreased. Often in those days, missionary songs would be sung in the services. One song in particular required me to make a real consecration just in order to sing it. We would sing, "Ready to go, ready to stay, ready my place to fill." With joy I would sing, "Ready to go"; but it took real surrender to sing, "Ready to stay." God was working within my heart a willingness to do His will whatever it was. I would find it to be quite important in the days ahead, for sometimes I would go and sometimes I would stay.

I had wonderful parents. Both my father and mother were very loving to me; but when I was 14 years old, they divorced. My father remarried a very nice lady while my mother remained single, and I lived with Mother. Since I had a missionary-minded mother, we often had missionary guests in our home. One particular lady named Juanita Boory stayed with us for a period of time. Listening to her tell of the child widows of India caused a stirring in my heart, and I felt a pull to that land; but I didn't yet know if it was God's will for me to go.

During one summer vacation about this time, Mother and I went to a conference in Seattle, Washington. After one of the services I knelt down and told God of my desire to go door-to-door to talk to people about Jesus. I said, "God, I would like to have someone go with me, but if you don't want to send someone to help me, I am willing to go alone." A few days after returning to Dallas, we received a phone call from someone

Juanita Boory

whom we had met just before the previous school year had ended. Dorothy Abercrombie had visited the church we were attending, and the pastor had asked if we could take her back to her dorm, for she was attending a university close to where we lived. Of course, we were happy to comply. Shortly afterward, Mother received a phone call from Dorothy, who said she had typhoid fever, so Mother visited her. She was supposed to be taking final exams, but it became necessary for her to return to her hometown as soon as she was able to travel. Those two times had been our only contacts with Dorothy. I hadn't even gone with Mother to visit her when she was sick, for I hadn't been particularly impressed with her at our first meeting.

School started again in the fall, and Dorothy returned to the university. Our phone rang again one day and I heard a very happy voice on the other end of the line. Dorothy was excitedly telling me that there had been a tent meeting during the summer in her small hometown, and she had accepted Jesus as her Lord and Savior. This was the beginning of a lifelong friendship between the two of us, as well as the answer to my prayer.

Not What I Expected!

Even though there was a three-year difference in our ages, we were like two peas in a pod. Dorothy became like a sister to me, and she would spend every weekend with us. We would both do our very best to get all of our homework done before the weekend, so we would have Saturdays free to go from house to house witnessing to people. Saturdays became the highlight of each week.

A year and a half later something happened that seemed to upset my apple cart. After church one night as Dorothy was praying, she fell on the floor under the power of the Holy Spirit. For about thirty minutes Mother and I waited for her while she lay on the floor in God's presence. When she finally arose, she said, "God has called me to Japan; I am going to quit going to the university at mid-term, so that I can go to Bible College instead. I felt like my world was crumbling before me. For quite a long time I had really desired to be a missionary, but God had never yet confirmed His will to me. All that I could see was that my best friend would be going away, and I would probably never see her again. I was broken-hearted. Mother tried to comfort me with the scripture, *"The lord gave, and the*

LORD *has taken away; blessed be the name of the LORD"*
(Job 1:21).

I tried to praise God in this heartbreaking situation, but it was very hard. This was a good time of surrender and consecration to the Lord for me. As it turned out, God wasn't taking my friend away from me as I thought; He was just leading her on to higher ground. She transferred to a Bible college that was only thirty miles away, and we continued to see each other almost every weekend. In fact, a year and a half later I graduated from high school and began attending the same college as Dorothy.

During that year in Bible College, Mother and I had some family friends who began telling us about a revival that God was sending to His church, and they invited us to attend the meetings. It turned out to be what is known as the "Latter Rain Revival." The Lord was supernaturally pouring out His Spirit in different places around the world, and one of the places happened to be in a small church near downtown Dallas. It was called the Dallas Gospel Center. As we visited the services from time to time, we enjoyed the presence of the Lord, and Mother became hungrier and hungrier for God.

We were still attending the church where we had received the baptism of the Holy Spirit, but Mother and I continued slipping out to visit the Dallas Gospel Center from time to time. Whenever our friends who first told us about the outpouring would try to convince us of the truth, I would begin to feel a great struggle inside. I knew that when I would try to witness about salvation to someone else, many times there would be a struggle between the flesh and the Spirit inside the person to whom I was witnessing. Now I realized that the same battle was going on inside of me. My reasoning was, "If I accept this new thing that God is doing, what will my relatives think? We have already left the conservative church we were attending and joined a Spirit-filled church. We have told all our relatives that we have found THE church. Now if we leave this church and go to another church, what will they think?" I would spend time in the college prayer room wrestling with God. If I had only known the blessings that awaited me, it wouldn't have taken me so long to surrender to His will.

Free!

Finally, one night near the end of the school year, I came to a place of decision. How clearly I remember the song the congregation was singing as I sat in the service at the Dallas Gospel Center. It went something like this.

> *"I am free; I am free.*
> *The blessed Holy Ghost*
> *in my heart is now the host.*
> *I am free."*

Suddenly, I knew that I was free. Free to believe . . . free to follow Jesus! It was a wonderful experience of surrender. As Mother and I drove back to the college that night, Dorothy was still in the sitting room of the dorm, as devotions there had just ended. She had no idea where I had been or what had happened to me, but she took one look at my face and knew something had changed. She came up to me and asked, "What happened to you?" Surrender to God had drastically changed my countenance.

Of course, Dorothy became hungry for what I had, so she began attending the services with us. She graduated from Bible College, and the time came for her to go home, but before she left, there was an important decision she had to make.

Detroit

During those final days of school we started attending the Dallas Gospel Center fairly regularly, for we were so blessed to be in the presence of God and the moving of His Spirit. There was such wonderful praise in the services, along with the operation of the gifts of the Spirit. I remember that even the announcements seemed to be anointed, for man was never exalted. All of our attention would be focused on God and His presence.

When God restored prophets and the gift of prophecy to the church, there began to be what we now refer to as presbytery—a group of prophets who would pray over an individual and give prophetic words to them that confirmed the gifts and ministry God had given that person.

When I was about fourteen years old, I started teaching children at church. Soon after we started attending the Dallas Gospel Center, the pastor's wife asked me if I would teach a children's class. Even though I had already been teaching a couple of years in our previous church, I was so hungry for God and felt so unable to teach until I really had God's calling made clear to me, that I refused. When we heard that people were coming from all over the world to be prayed over at Bethesda Temple in Detroit, Michigan, Mother decided that we would go. She invited Dorothy to go along. Dorothy really wanted to go, but she didn't know what to do, because her parents had not accepted the move of God. As Mother and I got on the bus to leave, Dorothy was still standing outside the bus trying to make up her mind. At the last minute, she boarded the bus, and we three left for Detroit.

Dorothy and Helen

After arriving and finding a place to stay in the home of one of the believers, we set ourselves to fast and pray. Every day we would stay at the church praying, and one night we never left the church. Each new day brought the hope that this would be the time when the prophets would call us out of the congregation and pray over us. Each day we sought to yield our will to God. After about ten days, the prophets called us up. As I went up for prayer and the proph-

"For we walk by faith, not by sight"—2 COR. 5:7 • **33**

ecies began, I felt clean inside and out. I have never felt so clean in my life. It was a wonderful feeling. Each day before that, I had felt that I was ready; but when the time really came, I realized that only then had I reached the place of full surrender. As the prophets prophesied, I heard what I had been waiting to hear: "You shall sow beside strange waters." God had accepted my desire to be a missionary!

That was a wonderful vacation for Mother, Dorothy and me. After God had spoken to us in prophecy, we went on to see Niagara Falls, Toronto and other places in the area. As we returned to Dallas, the time had come for Dorothy to go to her home and then to her place of ministry. The parting of our ways had come; but as always, God had more good things than we could dream of waiting ahead for us.

Chapter 9

To Go or Not To Go?

—Helen—

After having my ministry confirmed, I was once again ready to be active in the church. I also began making preparations to go to India when God opened up the way, for I felt like that was the land of my calling. In fact, Mother began buying material and having dresses made for me, so that I would have clothes ready when the time came. We had no idea what God really had in mind and how those clothes would ultimately be used! If we had known, some things would have been made quite differently.

With the end of that year approaching, I began to wonder if I should study Greek at Texas University in Austin, for I wanted to be able to understand Bible Greek. Also, I had never really been away on my own, for Mother had attended Bible College the same year that I had. I was now eighteen. After prayer and counsel from our pastor's wife, I made application to Texas University, but before I received an answer, something very strange happened.

Shortly before Christmas I went to spend a day or two with my father and his wife Pearl. They lived on the other side of town from Mother and me, so I had to ride more than one bus or streetcar to get to their house. I was always welcome in their home. Whenever I would go visit them, Dad would usually greet me at the door with his arms outstretched, waiting to give me a hug. On that particular night there was to be a Christmas service at the church. Now I never missed a service at the church whether it was rain or sunshine, snow or sleet, but this one time I had decided not to go. I thought it would be better to stay with my father and step-mother, but God had another plan. I began feeling that maybe I ought to go to church that night. I went to my room, knelt down on my knees and asked God to make His will plain to me. As I reasoned with God, He seemed to keep showing me that I should go, so I asked God why. His answer

"For we walk by faith, not by sight"—2 Cor. 5:7

was, "To minister to Brother Stanley." Brother Stanley was the same person I mentioned earlier in this book, and he had become the youth leader at the Dallas Gospel Center. He was a respected person in the church, but I had no idea why God gave me this answer. However, I decided to obey.

In order to reach church, I had to take a bus from a section known as Oak Cliff to downtown Dallas. There I needed to transfer to a streetcar that would take me to within a couple of blocks of the church. Imagine my surprise when I discovered that Brother Stanley was on the same streetcar I boarded! Well, since we were getting off at the same place, we ended up walking to church together. On the way, Brother Stanley asked me about what God had spoken to me when I had gone through presbytery, so I shared my calling and testimony with him briefly before we arrived at church, and that was the end of the matter. After the service ended and I arrived home, I had one question in my mind: "How had I ministered to Brother Stanley?" I would find out the following month.

The Proposal

In these days of the moving of God's Spirit, it wasn't uncommon to have special meetings that would last a week, two weeks, or even longer. Mother and I were at a service one Thursday morning in early January. After the service ended, Mother and I were at the door of the church preparing to leave when Brother Stanley, who also happened to be at the service, came up requesting to have a moment to talk with me. While Mother remained at the door talking to someone else, I followed Brother Stanley a few rows back until he decided on a place for us to sit. After safely depositing myself in a seat with one empty place between us, I turned to face him and hear what he had to say. Opening his mouth, he clearly stated his request: "I would like for you to pray about becoming my partner in the work of the Lord." As I answered, "All right," I noticed that Phil's lip was bleeding. I never knew whether his lip was cracked, or whether he had bitten it! To the best of my remembrance, that was the end of our conversation. Upon leaving the church, I asked my mother to pray for an unspoken request that I had. Her later confession was that she forgot to pray.

Early on in my Christian experience I had decided that I didn't want to go the way of spending my time playing love games with the other young people. I was interested in spending my time in a more profitable way; therefore, knowing the weakness of the flesh, I had cried out to God and asked Him to guide my life. In those days, it was often thought that it was a more spiritual thing for missionaries not to get married; so I didn't know if God wanted me to ever have a husband, or not. My prayer became, "Lord, please don't let me fall in love with anyone whom you don't want me to marry. If You want me to have a husband, please send him to me. If not, then You will be my husband." After my prayer, I tried my best to keep my mind focused on the Lord instead of the boys in the youth group. Probably because of this, I later learned that both my father and sister were afraid that I would end up being an old maid. I was still only eighteen!

After going home that eventful day, I set myself to fast and pray, for I really wanted to know God's will about the matter. Brother Stanley was the youth leader and a respected young man in the church, but I had never been with him except in the youth meetings, and since he had never even given me a special smile or any personal attention, I really didn't know him other than casually. He had been in our home only one time, when the whole youth group came for a time of snacks after an outreach service.

When Sunday arrived, a number of people stayed after the morning service to spend the afternoon in prayer for the evening meeting, and I was one of them; however, my main focus was this matter of finding an answer to the proposal that I had received. As the afternoon wore on, it seemed as though I was hearing God say to me, "Yes, marry Brother Stanley." In fact, there was one phrase that seemed to stand out to me in Hebrews 12:25: *"See that you do not refuse Him who speaks."* When I felt that God had said "Yes," I remember getting to my feet and going over to the other side of the church, for I had one thing that I wanted to ask the man who was kneeling there. As I approached him with my important question, I addressed him in the usual way. "Brother Stanley, what is your calling?" As he began telling me about his calling, I was intently listening for the word "India" but I wasn't hearing it. Finally, I came to myself enough to understand that he was telling me that he was called to the world! Having gained the information I needed, I politely said, "Thank you," and returned to my side of the church so that I could sort everything out with a little more prayer.

As the time drew near for the youth meeting to begin, I noticed that the youth leader got up to go unlock the door of the youth building behind the church. I followed him. Entering the hall, I walked up to him and said, "I think the Lord said, 'Yes.'"

He replied, "I thought so." And so our adventure began.

Chapter 10

Sweet Bliss

—Helen—

After the youth meeting ended, Phil (Oops—did I say Phil instead of Brother Stanley?) and I sat together in the church service for the first time. After service ended, I introduced Phil to my mother as her future son-in-law while we were still in the sanctuary. Her only question was, "Are you sure?" When I answered, "Yes," that seemed to be the end of the matter.

Mother and I soon left for home, where we had more time to talk. She informed me that she had intended to warn me when we reached home that evening that I needed to be careful, because Brother Stanley might be getting interested in me. We were engaged before she ever had a chance to give me that motherly advice! In fact, Mother was very happy and supportive about the whole matter.

I must admit that I was a bashful young person (as was Phil); but as soon as I said, "Yes" to him, I felt that I had known him all of my life, and I was very much in love! There seemed to be a perfect understanding between us whether we said anything or not.

A few days after this momentous occasion, I received a letter in the mail; I had been accepted at the university in Austin, Texas. Of course I now had no desire to leave for school, but since I had prayed about the matter and decided that was the direction the Lord wanted me to go, I felt I must go through with it. So, although lacking enthusiasm, Mother and I went to Austin to find a place for me to stay. Soon I was settled into a room in the home of a nice Christian lady who attended the same church that I planned to attend. My intention was to return home to Dallas about once a month, but my heart didn't agree with my mind. As each weekend arrived, I found myself on the train going home. Each time I went, I would expectantly wait for the moment when Phil would meet me at the train station and plant his first kiss on my lips. Time and time again I waited, and time and time again I only received a warm, loving greeting. It wasn't that there was no romance in our engagement, for there was. He and I would sit on the couch in the living room of Mother's home and just enjoy each other's presence. With his arm around me, we often felt no need even of conversation. As we would sit together, it seemed that the only thing that broke the silence was the loud ticking of his pocket watch!

It was a long block down to the park near Mother's house. Often we would take a walk down there so we could swing in the swings or feed the ducks in the pond. After some months had gone by, my dream finally became true; I received that first kiss for which I had been waiting.

Since our engagement had taken place in such a strange manner, we thought it was wisdom to let the people at the church think that we were just going together; so we only announced our engagement to our families. Since Phil had no extra money for an engagement ring, no one else really knew that we were engaged.

After finishing half a year in Austin, I decided to take a couple of subjects in Southern Methodist University, which was closer to our home in Dallas. That way I could live at home and be near Phil. In my sewing class I would listen to the other students describe the arguments and fights they had with their boyfriends or fiancés. It was hard for me to believe that people who were engaged could actually be fighting. I felt very sorry for them, for Phil and I never had any arguments during our engagement period, except for one small disagreement which took place the night before our wedding (and I don't even remember what that was about). Because of my experience, I guess I feel that couples who have arguments before marriage should carefully check to be sure that they are moving forward in God's will. Usually, people who argue before marriage only argue more after marriage.

As soon as we became engaged, I was expecting to get married right away, since God had confirmed His will to both of us. But Phil announced that we needed to wait for God's time. His plan was that we would check with each other at the beginning of each month to see what God had said. It wasn't until more than a year had passed that Phil said we would set our wedding date for April 12, 1952. This gave us plenty of time to get better acquainted.

Phil had already had some lessons concerning God's timing, for he had gotten ahead of the Lord in some previous decisions he had made. As he mentioned earlier, he had almost been engaged to a Jewish Christian girl in Pennsylvania. But when God showed him in a dream that he was about to make a mistake, he immediately broke up with her. That experience had been so vivid that he was afraid to pursue any girl again, unless he was sure she was the right one. That was why he prayed so long before saying anything to me.

Remember the time God told me to go to that Christmas program, and God had said that I was to go to encourage Brother Stanley? I didn't know he was actually considering proposing to me that very night, but God didn't give him the go-ahead signal until January. He told me that the first time he had seen me visit the church, he had felt impressed that I was to be his wife, but he had prayed over a year before asking me. All during the months that I had struggled in Bible College about whether or not to accept the move of God, Phil had been praying. God had prepared a good thing for both of us. By our both yielding to God's dealing in our lives, we had been brought together.

Another hard lesson Phil received was when he tried to go out in ministry ahead of time. His self-effort resulted in failure and the accumulation of a debt. At that time God had spoken to him saying, "Take a lower seat, and then I will bring you up higher."

Grace Gospel Church

Before I ever met Phil, a friend told him about a church in Waco, Texas. His friend had said, "They have all nine gifts of the Spirit in operation there." Of course that had made Phil more than ready to investigate. After he arrived in Waco, he found the Grace Gospel

Church about which his friend had spoken. Even though the church itself was just a very small white wooden building, he discovered that the pastor, his wife and family were very loving and hospitable; the best part was that the Spirit of the Lord was moving there in a special way just like in other parts of the country. Glenn Ewing and his wife, often referred to as Mom and Dad Ewing, received Phil with open arms.

It wasn't long after Phil and I were engaged that the Ewings started having conventions, later known as The Homecoming—and that is just what they were. Mother and Phil attended the first convention, but I was unable to do so. My sister had her first baby just then, and I went to help her. That first convention was a week long, but later it was narrowed down to two shorter conventions, held each year just before Easter, and in October just before the Fall Equinox.

Chapter 11

Finally Married!

—Helen—

The day for our wedding finally arrived. On Saturday, April 12, 1952, Phil and I were married at the church. We had a simple wedding with a few of our family and friends attending. We had no attendants, but my brother-in-law gave me away. Our songs were "Blest Be the Tie That Binds" and "He Leadeth Me." During the wedding Phil had allowed me to put his wedding ring on the wrong hand, even though it was too small for that finger. All the way to the reception, he was trying to get the ring off so he could put it on the right hand. Even though he ended up with a bloody finger, he finally accomplished his purpose. After a reception at Mother's home, we left on our honeymoon.

Phil had taken two or three days off work so we could drive to Waco, about 100 miles away. Mother offered to let us use her car for the trip. Our plan was to attend the end of a convention. Our first meal together was actually a foretaste of our traveling days to come: cheese and crackers that we quickly bought in a grocery store on the way to Waco! I think we did stop at a roadside park long enough to eat our bountiful meal. Actually, we both enjoyed it immensely.

The highlight of the conventions in Waco was always the Saturday night communion and foot washing at the end of the service. Arriving just in time for the foot washing, Phil went with the men and I with the ladies. As we compared notes afterwards, we found out that Pastor Glenn Ewing had washed Phil's feet while prophesying over him and Mom Ewing had washed mine. We both felt quite honored. Besides that, Dad Ewing had asked Phil to preach the next morning. I felt blessed as a newly-wed to sit and listen to my husband give his first message since our marriage.

The next two days went all too quickly. Soon it was time for Phil to return to work. We drove back to my mother's home in Dallas, for Mother had said we could live with her.

Right at the beginning of our marriage we made an agreement that would serve us well in the days ahead. We decided that instead of arguing and fighting, we would get down on our knees together and pray if a disagreement arose between us. In fact, we agreed that we would not get up from our knees until we had apologized to each other and made everything right. With God's help, we kept our word. This led to our spending much time in prayer in the early years of our marriage. Even though I was greatly in love with my husband and never ever wanted to be even one room away from him, there were many times that I would get my feelings hurt and start to cry. We had many adjustments to make, but prayer got us safely through each problem, even though at times our meals would be delayed an hour or so. Everything had to be put on hold until we had apologized and things were straightened out between us.

It wasn't long before I began feeling sick, for our first son would be born nine months and ten days after our wedding. (I might have gotten pregnant earlier in our marriage, if we had been able to figure out the lovemaking procedure sooner, but we have never regretted the fact that we were both ignorant before marriage, for this gave us a real sense of trust in each other.)

We were living on a shoestring, for Phil's salary was very small. I learned how to make good eggless cakes and pancakes. One day as I walked home from the grocery store I was fairly skipping with a real song in my heart, for I could hardly wait to show Phil that I had been able to buy several different kinds of meat to eat for the coming week. Chicken and Dumplings was one of his favorite dishes, and I had managed to buy four small chicken necks for the special price of four cents for all four!

Phil always has taken the ministry of the Word very seriously. One night everyone was invited to a special gathering at the church. We usually attended everything, but Phil had decided that we wouldn't go that night, because he was supposed to preach at church the next night, so he needed to prepare. As the time grew closer for the meeting to begin, Mother kept urging us to go. After this went on for some time, Mother finally said, "The church is giving you a surprise wedding shower tonight, and it has already started." Upon hearing this, I began insisting that we should go, but it still took some effort to convince Phil that the shower (in this case) was more important than his preparation for ministry. We finally arrived close to the end of the shower and the money that the people had been waiting to give to us was a great blessing!

Does God Have a Car for Us?

After a few months Mother told us she would buy us a new car. As Phil prayed about the offer, God said, "I don't want you to have a new car; I want you to have a 1948 Buick." At the same time, God impressed him that he would find the Buick at Strayhorn-Lacy. That was the name of a car dealer in Oak Cliff on the other side of Dallas.

On our first free day, we expectantly boarded a streetcar and got off close to Strayhorn-Lacy. As we walked into the showroom, guess what we saw? A beautiful, black 1948 Buick. As we inspected it closely, we saw that it was in tip-top condition both inside and out, plus it had only been owned by one person, a car dealer. It was the perfect answer to our prayers—the car of our dreams—but as we were talking, suddenly a man got in the car and drove away. Someone had beaten us to the sale! However, with a confession of faith Phil said, "Helen, the Lord could still give us that car even though someone else bought it."

Still it was with a down-hearted spirit that we walked away from the lot toward the streetcar stop. We had just missed God's plan by minutes it seemed. Suddenly Phil felt that God said, "Don't get the streetcar here, but cross the street and walk down to the next streetcar stop. Phil said, "I think that we shouldn't get on the streetcar here; I feel that we should go down to the next streetcar stop," So onward we walked. We saw another used car lot across the street, so we unenthusiastically decided to go there to look. There was a 1948 Buick there, too; but compared to the other one, it was junk. As we were walking on to the next streetcar stop, we noticed a car parked in the parking lot of a barbeque restaurant. Phil said, "Look! That is just like the car God wanted us to have!" The next thing we saw was a man leaning out the window. He asked, "Did you want to buy this car?" We said, "Yes, we really did." The man answered, "Well, if you want it, jump in the car with me and I'll take you to my shop. You can have it for the same price I paid for it. I am a car dealer, and I was just buying it to put on my lot to sell." As it turned out, the man was a Christian. All the time we had spent looking at the junk Buick at the second car lot, he had been waiting for us. Not only that, if we had caught a streetcar at the first stop, we might have missed him. We were very thankful for our beautiful new car; however, it wasn't long before we were to learn a very hard lesson that would involve the car. Before going into that, though, I would like to tell you more about my friend Dorothy.

Chapter 12

Ahead of Me!

—Helen—

After Phil's dramatic proposal, I wrote a letter to Dorothy to tell her I was engaged. Imagine my chagrin when some time later Dorothy wrote back and told me that she was married. I thought that I had one on her, but she had gotten engaged and married while I was still waiting to be married. It just didn't seem right that she would beat me to it. As it turned out, however, a young, fiery evangelist named Ray Jennings had come through town and won her heart all in a matter of about three weeks!

Not long after we were married, Ray and Dorothy came through Dallas. Mother and I had the opportunity to meet Ray, but Phil was at work. Like me, Dorothy had become pregnant soon after her wedding. Even though we tried to persuade our friends to stay longer, they insisted that they needed to get on their way. Ray had received his draft notice for the military, and they had a deadline to meet. With a feeling of sadness, we bid them goodbye. Later we heard that Ray had gone to the induction center and gone through all of the necessary preliminary steps, but as he was about to be sworn in, he suddenly remembered to tell them that his wife was pregnant. A few minutes later he walked away from the induction center free to return to his wife and continue the evangelistic ministry.

A Special Homecoming

We looked forward to the conventions each year. It would be a great time of enjoying the presence of the Lord, receiving a refreshing, and having fellowship with friends. Mom

Dad Glenn Ewing

"For we walk by faith, not by sight"—2 Cor. 5:7

and Dad Ewing were like spiritual parents to us. Even though the Dallas Gospel Center was our home church and the place that Phil trained for the ministry, we received much in Waco. Before we came in contact with the Ewings, I would often go to the altar to be saved whenever an invitation was given, but the day came when I realized that I had been saved by the blood of Jesus; God wasn't going to throw me out of His Kingdom just because I made some mistakes, any more than I was going to throw out our own children when they failed to be perfect.

As I came to understand that we are made up of spirit, soul and body, I realized there is also a three-fold salvation for us. God does His part by living in our spirit, but He expects us to take care of our soul by yielding our wills to Him. Philippians 2:12–13 says, *"Therefore, my beloved, as you have always obeyed, not as in my presence only, but now much more in my absence, work out your own salvation with fear and trembling; for it is God who works in you both to will and to do for His good pleasure . . ."* He wants to make it easy for us by putting His desires in our heart. As we allow the Holy Spirit to work in our lives, we become more and more like Jesus and we grow in Him. This truth was very liberating to me as I realized that I was God's child for all eternity. It also brought a greater love to my heart and a rest to my soul, because I loved God and wanted to please Him. Now I was able to serve Him because of love instead of fear!

The Homecoming in October, 1952 was special. I happened to be in the sanctuary when Robert Ewing (the Ewings' son) announced, "The Jennings have just arrived." I could scarcely believe my ears as I asked Robert to repeat what he had just said. When I realized he really meant Ray and Dorothy, I jumped up to run and meet them. As soon as Phil was introduced to Ray, the two of them disappeared to get acquainted and talk about the things of the Lord. It was clear to see from that moment on that the two of them were like brothers—opposites, but able to complement one another in the ministry. That was the opening to the next phase of our lives, which would include ministering off and on with the Jennings for the next ten years. What was it that I had thought when Dorothy had been called to the mission field that night a few years earlier? I had thought that I would never see her again, and that God was taking her away from me. Truly, God's ways are past finding out. In fact, after the morning that Phil had proposed to me a few years earlier, I remember testifying about Isaiah 55:8–9: "*For My thoughts are not your thoughts, Nor are your ways My ways,*" says the Lord. "*For as the heavens are higher than the earth, So are My ways higher than your ways, And My thoughts than your thoughts.*" It is amazing how wise God is! "*Oh the depth of the riches both of the wisdom and knowledge of God! How unsearchable are His judgments, and His ways past finding out!*" (Rom. 11:33). God had only separated Dorothy and me for a time that He might further prepare us and let us each find our mates. So often we think that God is taking something away from us, when in reality He is only preparing something better for us. "How did you happen to come to this convention?" I asked Ray and Dorothy.

"God just told us to come to Waco; we didn't know there was going to be a convention," they replied.

Ray's brother Jim, and his wife June were with Ray and Dorothy. They were all excited about the special victory God had given them in the birth of their last child. June had given birth previously by C-section, but the last baby had been delivered naturally by a midwife. Now the use of a midwife was almost never heard of in those days, but Phil was greatly impressed by their testimony and announced to me that we were going to have a midwife deliver our baby. I was far from enthusiastic when I first heard this, but little by little I was won over. It was only about three months now until our firstborn was due; but the big question uppermost in our minds was, "Where was he to be born?"

Chapter 13

A Sweet Addition

—Helen—

Our desire and goal was to be in ministry. When Ray and Dorothy came through Dallas in December on their way to minister at a church in Nebraska, they invited us to go along. After prayer, we jumped at the opportunity. Phil was able to take a short leave from his job. The Jennings were accompanied by their newborn son, Philip, and by Ray's brother, Jim, along with his wife and children. One other lady with her children went, too, for they all planned to go to see their relatives in Vashon Island, Washington, after the ministry in Nebraska was over.

What a wonderful time we had with the Whittingtons in Nebraska, and how good it was to be in the work of the Lord; we were hooked by the delights of the ministry. During the meetings the Jennings began inviting us to go on to Washington with them so we could meet Ray's family and see beautiful Vashon Island. As the lure of travel took over, we all started out together in two cars; but it wasn't long before we came to a crossroad. There was a sign pointing to Dallas. When Phil saw that sign, God spoke to him saying that he should turn there and return home. Phil shared God's leading with me, but I was of no mind to return home, for I was having the time of my life. At that point, all the others began begging us to go on with them. Including all of the children, there were fifteen people in the Jennings's car, so they really needed our car to help them. Yielding to pressure, Phil decided to continue onward with the group. We were about to learn a lasting lesson about following the leading of the Spirit. In fact, one time we had talked to our pastor's wife in Dallas about whether it was better for a minister to work or to live by faith. She had told us that we needed to find out God's plan for our own personal lives. It would be fine to work, if that was God's leading; or, it would be fine to be full time and just trust God to supply. If we chose to be full time, it would be more important than ever to walk in God's will. She and her husband had learned through experience that God would provide for His will, but if someone chose to walk in their own will, they would suffer. We found that advice to be very true!

As we headed to Washington, we had gone only a short distance up the road when the Jennings' car broke down. The bad news was that it was beyond repair. The only alternative was for all fifteen people in the Jennings's car to pile into our car. When the transfer was completed, we foolishly continued on our way.

Since it was wintertime and snow was on some of the roads, we ran into trouble one night. We had no chains (and no money). The car just couldn't make it up one steep, icy hill. We couldn't go up nor could we turn around. All of our efforts to push the car only ended in getting the car turned halfway around and in the ditch, so that we were parked across one side of the two-lane highway with our rear end against the mountain and our car facing a high drop-off just across the adjoining lane. Fortunately, we had enough gas in the car to run the heater all night long; but each time a truck would come up or down the mountain, we would pray that they would be able to get by without hitting us. It was with much thanksgiving and joy that we greeted the man with the snow plow that came to pull us out the next morning.

Our time in Vashon was interesting, but it was very cold, and we had another big problem. Before arriving in Washington, our car had begun to make noise. Now we learned that the grease seal had broken the night we had gone into the ditch on the side of the mountain. Our biggest predicament was that our baby was due very soon, so we needed to get home quickly. After doing our best to get the car patched up, fervent prayer was made by all that the Lord would send a Chinook wind and clear the highway before us from Washington to Texas. A merciful, kind loving Father heard our prayer and sent a warm Chinook wind that cleared the road from Washington to Dallas. Ray, Dorothy, Baby Philip, Phil and I were able to drive nonstop back home. We arrived home on January 20th. After a night's rest, I spent the next day washing clothes.

"For we walk by faith, not by sight"—2 Cor. 5:7

Before going to bed that night, Ray and Dorothy were in our room visiting. They happened to mention nonchalantly that they had had some special meetings in a small town in East Texas called Overton, about 120 miles from Dallas. After Ray and Dorothy left the room, Phil and I looked at each other and said, "Overton is where we are supposed to have our baby!" Up until that time, we hadn't known where our baby should be born. There were only two things we did know. One was that we were going to have a midwife, and the other was that the baby would be born in a small town not far from Dallas. Happy that we finally knew the answer, we went to bed, but about midnight, I began feeling labor pains. By eight o'clock the next morning, I knew something had to be done. The car needed to be fixed, but I was about to have a baby.

After sharing with the Jennings our feelings about Overton, Dorothy said she would call the pastor to see if there was a midwife there. The pastor said he didn't know, but he would look for one. After a brief conversation with the pastor, Dorothy hung up the phone and reported that a midwife was available. (She didn't mention that he was only going to look for one). Without losing time, we all jumped in the car and Mother began driving the one hundred and ten miles to Overton. I lay down in the back seat, with Phil squeezing in between the seats the best he could. During this time I learned the healing power of the Word of God, for Phil was faithfully reading scripture to me while I was in labor. As the pains increased, I closed my eyes. Phil, thinking that I was asleep, ceased reading. When the scripture reading stopped, the pain felt so much worse. I wanted to ask him to continue reading, but didn't feel I could talk without screaming; so I remained silent for the remainder of the trip.

The pastor had located a midwife; so as soon as we arrived at the parsonage, the pastor jumped in his car to get her. Shortly afterward, the pastor returned with a kind, grandmotherly-looking black Baptist lady who knew how to pray. With everyone else in the house praying, too, the remaining hour and a half went by quickly.

During the delivery, Mother was standing by the side of the bed with a worried look on her face, but the pastor's wife had a joyful look of anticipation. Every time I looked at Mother, the pain grew worse, but when I looked at the face of the pastor's wife, the pain lessened. I realized that we could encourage one another by our facial expressions.

Jonathan David made his appearance into this world on January 22, 1953. (God had given Phil his name before he was born.) It was a joyous experience and one that I would never have wanted to change, for the presence of the Lord was there in such a mighty manner, and a stream of praise to God in tongues poured out from my innermost being as our son came forth. Even Mother became a staunch supporter of home delivery after that.

As our son was placed in my arms, I noticed a little bump on his right ear in the very spot where Phil had a bump on his right ear. Truly, "we are fearfully and wonderfully made." God had put an identification mark on Jonathan—he was officially a Stanley!

Before long I learned why God had sent us to this specific place for the birth. The pastor's wife soon came to my bedside and requested that I pray for them to have another child. Seven years earlier she had been put through a terrible experience at the hospital where their only son had been born, so she had never wanted to give birth again. After watching my delivery, she was delivered from her fear. We prayed, and about nine months later the Lord gave that couple a lovely little girl.

The Ladds with their son and us.

After nursing Jonathan, we laid him in the doll buggy that the pastor and his wife had prepared for us. Then the pastor happily announced, "Hey, we have two evangelists here; let's start some special meetings tonight." I wasn't able to go to service the first two nights, but since the church was just next door to the parsonage, I crawled out of bed on Sunday morning in time to go over for the preaching. At the close of the service, we dedicated Jonathan to the Lord, and God spoke concerning him in prophecy. He was three days old.

Chapter 14

Can God Provide for Three, Too?

—Helen—

Phil and I began having family altar together as soon as we were married. When our son was born, we immediately included him in our prayer and reading of the Word, for we wanted him to have the same heritage that we had enjoyed.

Returning to Dallas after the meeting was over, our attention once again had to be focused on the car. Even though we had it fixed, it was never quite the same again. We had gotten out of God's will and had to pay the consequences. God let us go through a time of great financial leanness. There followed a period of real repentance. By the time God again opened the door of ministry for us, we were more serious than ever about wanting to follow in God's footsteps; but we had many lessons yet to learn.

God was helping me to learn to live by faith. I had been taught to tithe as a child, but I had never really needed to believe God for my daily needs. Even though there had been a time when our family was so poor that Daddy, Mother and Marian had lived in a tent at the job Dad was doing, things had been going better for my parents by the time I came along. I remember one time when I was still in elementary school, Daddy told me he was going to increase my allowance to twenty-five cents, but I answered saying, "I have enough; I don't need anymore." Daddy took me at my word and never offered to increase it again. Many times after that I wondered why I had made such a foolish statement, but I never asked for more. If I had asked, I'm sure he would have gladly raised my allowance. God tells us to "Ask and you shall receive." Sometimes we just don't ask, and that's why we don't receive.

Since Phil had grown up in much poverty, he was more experienced in believing God to supply his needs. We began to see many ways that God was helping us, but there was one definite experience that helped increase my faith. Someone had given us some used baby clothes. Among them was a nice little blue outfit. Since blue was

my favorite color, it was a real test for me when I thought I heard God tell me to give that outfit to someone else. I struggled with God for a while, but at last I surrendered and gave it away. It wasn't long afterwards that I received a package in the mail. When I opened it, out fell the exact same blue outfit. The only difference was that it was new and not faded!

Launching Out

As the months went by, we learned that the Ladds—the pastors of the church in Overton in whose home Jonathan had been born—were going to move, and the church would be without a pastor. We had kept close contact with the Ladds and the church, who were all very dear to our hearts. The Jennings and we decided to go spend some time helping the church. During our time together, the Jennings presented us with a new challenge. They had been somewhere and learned the blessing of spending time praising God without asking Him for anything. They said, "Do you know that it is very difficult to even pray a few minutes without finding yourself making a request to God?" Finding this to be true, we set about trying to train ourselves differently. Every morning we began having a two-hour prayer meeting at the church. The first hour was filled with nothing but praise and worship; then we would present our requests to God. This proved to be so wonderful that it became a daily pleasure for a period of time.

During this time together in Overton, God began speaking to us concerning the mission field. We started to feel that God's time had come for us to go to India, and the Jennings felt the pull of God to England; so it was decided that we would return to our respective homes and prepare to leave in December.

We were able to get enough money together for one-way tickets, and Mother bought us a jeep station wagon to take. I began giving all of our things away, for I did not know when or if we would ever return, but Mother wisely kept most of the things for when we returned. The church prayed over us, and we began our trip to San Francisco to board our ship. However, we didn't yet have our visa for India.

Things didn't look good for us at the Indian Consulate. They said they would not give us a visa unless we had our return tickets. Of course, we had no money for return tickets, so that sounded impossible. No manner of persuasion seemed to sway the officials, so we returned to our hotel room for the night. The next morning we arose and began our hour of praise. Soon the telephone rang and a voice on the other end of the line said, "Come pick up your visas." God had performed a miracle through praise. We picked up our visas and hardly had time to make it to the ship. (Travel by ship was much cheaper than by air in those days.) We had barely been able to find a space on a ship, so we ended up leaving First Class on the American President Line. The ship was named President Cleveland. Our mothers were both on hand to tell us goodbye as we set sail in 1953. The ship first sailed to Los Angeles before heading out to sea.

We had just entered our cabin and sat down to our first meal when the ship began to move; immediately I began feeling sick. Actually, I spent much of my time in bed resting for the first few weeks of the journey.

Chapter 15

The Voyage

—Helen—

After four days we arrived in Honolulu. Since we were on a passenger ship, we would have a few hours to disembark and see some sights at every stop. As we were going down the gangplank in sunny Hawaii, there was a taxi driver at the bottom who said something to us. Thinking surely we had not heard correctly, we listened again to what he was saying. Was he really saying, "Hallelujah! Praise the Lord!?" Upon questioning him we found out that we had heard correctly—after only one look at us, he had known we were missionaries. This experience was wonderful to me, for my parents had always been very hospitable. If mother had a guest, she was always very careful to pack a lunch for them before they went on their way the next day. Now we found that God was taking care of us, her children, in the same way she had taken care of others, and He had sent a special messenger to meet us at the very first port.

Since for a time before our marriage Phil had worked in a grocery store produce department, he had a real interest in grocery stores. Our first sightseeing trip in Honolulu was a grocery store—not to buy anything, but just to see what the store looked like. In the years that have followed, we have gone to tour grocery stores around the world. We did take time to visit the aquarium in Honolulu; we laughed to see Jonathan try to put his hand in the fishes' mouths, even though there was a glass separating him from them.

It took two weeks to reach Japan. The waters were especially rough in that area, but sailing was a little better after leaving there. Since Phil had been in the military in Japan, we decided to try to visit an elderly pastor whom he had known. The weather was cold and damp in Yokohama, but the streets of Tokyo were decorated with large posters of Uncle Sam dressed as Santa Claus hanging over each intersection. Having nothing but an address, we set out to see if we could find the pastor's house. We showed the address to someone who spoke no English. After looking at the address, the man beckoned us to follow him. Silently he led us to the train station, paid for tickets for himself and us, and boarded the train with us. In about an hour he directed us to alight from the train. We continued to follow him down different paths until we reached the pastor's home. At that point, our guide suddenly left. We still had not been able to communicate with him. What an example of Japanese courtesy this was to us! It made us wonder if we Americans would ever do such a nice thing for a stranger. As the years went by, we learned that the Japanese and those in various other countries were much more polite in many ways than we or our fellow Americans usually are.

Christmas

We were on board the ship when Christmas arrived. A big masquerade party was given on Christmas Eve, and a prize was given out to the best-dressed passenger. Even though we had no desire to attend the party, we were curious to know who the prize winner was. The next morning we found our answer. A different clergyman was allowed a free trip on each voyage, so that there would always be a clergyman on board, if there was a need for one. The clergyman on this voyage was often bleary-eyed, from spending much time in the bar. He turned out to be the winner—dressed as the devil!

Each passenger received a gift. Ours was a silver cigarette lighter, which we threw overboard. In afterthought, I guess we could have gotten some money for the silver, but we had no desire to keep a cigarette lighter.

One highlight of this trip was that Jonathan stood by himself for the first time as we were sailing across the ocean. He didn't really begin to walk until his friend, Philip Jennings, arrived in India a few months later.

Hong Kong

We were able to have friendship and prayer with a couple of the passengers, one of whom was a Finnish missionary the Communists had expelled from his mission station in China. The ship stopped at the Philippines before arriving in Hong Kong. Here we were to change to a British passenger liner, but it involved a four-day wait, during which time we were able to meet some of the Christians in the area and even attend a Brethren service on Sunday morning. In that service was a couple who were returning from their mission field in Burma. The man gave his testimony about how he had been traveling on horseback in a robber-infested area when a band of robbers came to attack him. It seems that the Spirit of the Lord suddenly took over and he began wielding his whip and loudly speaking in tongues. The robbers fled! He didn't know whether he was speaking in their language or not, but whatever happened, the Lord took care of the situation.

Another very stirring, impressive event was the opportunity to hear Geoffrey Bull speak. He had just been released after spending three years in a Communist prison, and had walked past the Bamboo Curtain into freedom a few hours earlier. He later wrote a book concerning his ministry, but at the time we heard him, he testified about how the Lord had clearly given him the scripture Joshua 1:11, *"Pass through the camp and command the people, saying, 'Prepare provisions for yourselves, for within three days you will cross over this Jordan, to go in to possess the land which the Lord your God is giving you to possess.'"* When God impressed that scripture upon him, he understood that God was talking about reading the Bible; so for three days, he hungrily devoured the Word of God. After three days, he was taken captive and his Bible was taken away. For three years he had no access to the Bread of Life. Three years to the very day after he had been captured, he was released from prison and became a free man! God was teaching us many things on this first missionary journey—things that we have stored away in our hearts throughout the years.

We had the opportunity to be driven to a place that was right by the border of Communist China. I can still remember looking over into what seemed to be a beautiful, green, mountainous country and thinking how sad it was that the enemy had taken into bondage so many precious souls.

Moving On

All too soon the four days ended, and once again we were bound for India on the British P. & O. ship line. The ship stopped at Singapore, Penang and Colombo before arriving in Bombay. The waters were calmer after leaving Hong Kong, and I had become well rested after all of my forced rest. The cruise was so enjoyable that I hardly wanted to get off the boat when we finally reached our destination. Since the meal hour for children on the ship was before the main meal time, it was interesting to be with all of the other British mothers who gathered to feed their young children. I became accustomed to coddled eggs, jelly (jello), cream ices and other English delicacies.

The Church of England Sunday morning service was held on the deck with the breeze gently blowing. It was a wonderful feeling. The sailors and the passengers were there in their Sunday best as we sang together the stirring hymn, "*The Church's one foundation is Jesus Christ our Lord....*" It was as though I could envision the whole body of Christ worshipping together. Even then God was trying to help me understand that no church has it all—all born-again Christians are part of the wonderful and mysterious body of Christ, and it is so sweet to have fellowship together. There is no better place than the mission field to realize this, for fellowship with other Christians is often quite a luxury if you are in a place where churches and Christians are few.

We had the opportunity to get off the boat in Ceylon (now Sri Lanka) for a few hours; we met up with a missionary who took us to visit a Bible school there, then we sailed on until we landed in Bombay, India—the land of my dreams!

India at Last!

As we left the ship, we left behind our place of security that we had enjoyed for five weeks. Now we were on our own. In January of 1954 we arrived in India with a car, two or three addresses, and a hotel reservation at the Sea Green Hotel, located along the seashore.

When filling out our customs form, I carefully listed each item along with the price; however since we had various things made from plastic, I just carelessly lumped them all together as plastic ware and wrote down one price. How dismayed I was when we were charged 100% duty on the plastic ware. A person never knows what to expect, for each country is different. We learned later that India had started making little plastic trinkets, and so they didn't want any competition being brought from abroad. That was the only duty we were charged, besides the huge duty on the car. (Maybe taking a car to India wasn't such a good decision after all!) When we received our car, we were almost amused to see that simple things like a little red light on the dashboard and the rotor in the distributer were missing: they weren't things of value—just something that had caught the eye of some poor person. Because of sitting so long without use, the diaphragm in the carburetor had dried out and had to be replaced before we could drive the car.

Chapter 16

Duped

—Philip—

Phil and I in Bombay

The days at the hotel were interesting. The elevator would only take you up, but you had to walk down. The food was delicious and the service superb, but our real purpose in being there was to determine what our next step would be. We had two addresses of people we had met in America. They both lived far away and we didn't feel any leading to contact them. There was one person whom we did contact, even though he, too, lived quite a distance away. That contact had graduated from the Dallas Theological Seminary. He came to visit us at the hotel and took us to meet a famous evangelist named Bakht Singh, who was known as the Billy Graham of India. We enjoyed meeting Bakht Singh, but nothing special came out of the visit. The only thing we knew to do was to set our hearts to seek the Lord. A few days had passed when an unexpected visitor arrived at our door. We invited him in, and he introduced himself to us as a brother in Christ. As we listened to him speak, we heard him say, "You are just the man I am looking for. I will open many doors for you." He invited us to come with him to church on Sunday morning, so we agreed to go.

—Helen—

He arrived bright and early on Sunday, and we accompanied him to church. After arriving, it seemed like everyone was supposed to wash clean and change into white clothes before entering the service. We were given some kind of white cloth with which to cover our heads. During the process of the service, we were called up to the front and asked to kneel. A man began prophesying over us. At that point, we could take no more. Phil and I jumped up and almost ran out of the place, for we realized that we had been duped into attending something connected to a cult. It seemed that among other things, they believed in fire-walking.

Kurien Joseph

This experience taught us another lesson. Sometimes the false comes before the true, for it wasn't long after that until a real servant of the Lord appeared at our hotel door. Kurien Joseph was a real spirit-filled servant of God who was used to open more doors in India than we were ever able to enter; he even went with us to some of the places to help us get started.

Before we started out in ministry away from Bombay, though, there was one more time that we were tricked. One day a man named Mr. Cole came to see us with a gracious invitation to come stay at his house with his family. Since our pockets were not overflowing with money, and since hotels can be costly, we accepted his invitation and cancelled the remaining part of our hotel reservation. As soon as we had climbed up the many flights of stairs to the third floor carrying Jonathan (and being accompanied by others who were carrying our trunks on their heads), we realized that we had made the wrong decision. The apartment was very small with no running water, and we were squeezed into one small room, for the rest of the small space was occupied by Mr. Cole's family, which included several children. All of the water had to be carried by hand up the stairs, and Jonathan was still in diapers. (In those days there were no such things as disposable diapers; each diaper had to be washed out by hand.) We learned to take a bath with a few cups of water, and it seemed like I was only using thimblesful of water to wash diapers. To cap it all, every day Mr. Cole would approach us for some money to buy groceries for us and his entire family! We would go to bed at night dreaming of the wonderful meals that we had left behind at the Sea Green Hotel, for it was quite evident that it was Cole and his family who were receiving a blessing—not us!

Our first trip to India took us to all of the places on the map except Warangal, Calcutta and Delhi. We went to villages, as well. Since then, we've been to many other areas.

"For we walk by faith, not by sight"—2 Cor. 5:7

Chapter 17

Following Jesus

—Helen—

Jonathan and Phil

The day came for us to leave Bombay and begin the traveling ministry for which we had come. Setting out in our jeep armed with our Bibles, some simple faith, water purifying tablets, mosquito repellent, two sleeping bags and a Coleman camp stove, we had lots to learn; but God was so gracious to us.

Whenever Indians traveled, they took their bed rolls with them, so we were quite in style with our sleeping bags. The scripture, "He took up his bed and walked," took on new meaning. I had always pictured a man carrying a bed, but then I realized that it was only a mat or bedroll that he carried. As for the purifying tablets, we tried to slip them into our drinks as unobtrusively as possible, not wanting to offend our hosts. Citronella was our mosquito repellent. Since it only lasted two hours, the mosquitos would nicely remind us when it ran out, so we would wake up and rub some more of the awful smelling liquid on our bodies. Many of the places had no electricity; this meant that there were no fans either. Most of the kitchen vessels were made of brass, and even the telephone poles were of brass, too.

Our first stop was Poona (now Pune). In India it is common for

Christians to choose a Bible name to use after their conversion, for their original names often have to do with Hinduism. Since their method of naming is different from ours, you cannot tell who is akin to whom by their names, for they go by what we would consider their first names. Another custom is that the wives don't sit down to eat with their husbands. In fact, often the man of the house doesn't even sit down with the guests. The guests eat first while the host or hostess serves. In Poona the pastor proudly told us that he ate with his wife, so it was a blessing for all of us to sit down and eat together. His name was Yeshudian, which he explained meant "Follower of Jesus".

Our next stop was Sholapur wher had evangelistic meetings with Pastor Kuruvilla and his sister. After we finished praying for the sick one time, Pastor Kuruvilla said, "Let's have a love feast." Now this presented a problem to me, for having a love feast meant to kiss each other, and the way the Indian churches kissed each other was to plant a kiss on each cheek. Since we had just finished praying for some lepers to be healed, I wondered, "Does this mean I should kiss the lepers for whom we just prayed, too?" After consideration, I concluded that it did, even though it sorely tested my faith!

The time spent with Pastor Kuruvilla began a lifelong friendship with him. When we returned to Sholupur many years later, he was married, and we were greatly impressed by his wife, their three daughters and one son. Pastor Kuruvilla has gone to be with the Lord; but we are still friends with the rest of the family, most of whom live in the States now.

The temperature was becoming hotter and hotter. By the time we reached Sholupur, people had begun saying, "You had better go to the mountains or hills until the weather gets cooler." But God was saying to Phil, "Preach the gospel!" That's when God gave him the key to the problem and launched him on the adventures of dominion over the weather. Since the hot season was from March through May, we had a good long period of time to prove God's Word. This was the key that God gave him. "Pray for a shower of rain the night before you are to travel; then believe God for a cloud-covering during the trip." This would take a miracle, for it's not supposed to rain in the dry (hot) season, but God really proved Himself. Every trip we took after that was preceded by a shower of rain the night before and a cloud-covering during the trip. I said every trip; but there was one exception which I can later explain.

Our third major stop was Hyderabad. As we were traveling along the "highway" toward Hyderabad that day in 1953, I began to feel sick; the closer we came to Hyderabad, the more I came to the realization that I was pregnant again! This brought quite a change of events.

Considering the fact that I had grown up in a family that didn't even put pepper on the table at meal time, and for sure they didn't use chilies in the food, it had been a step of faith for me to go to India. To be truthful, the first time I had ever even eaten a bowl of chili was when I was in Bible College. Launching out into the realm of unknown tastes, I had determined that if I were going to be a missionary, I had better learn to eat whatever was set before me, and that included chili. I had passed that test. Now when I found myself in India, the food proved to be a real challenge, for there was almost nothing that was served us that was not burning hot with red chilies. This included even breakfast eggs or the mid-afternoon snacks that would be served us with the tea. I had found one consolation—the delicious tortilla-like bread that was called chapatti was made with no chilies. Now when I became pregnant, you guessed it; my stomach began to rebel against chapattis. James 4:6 says, *"But he gives more grace",* and He did.

Pastor Abraham and his Family

We fell in love with Pastor Abraham and his family there in Hyderabad. They, too, became our lifelong friends until Pastor Abraham and his wife were called home to be with the Lord. Twice Pastor Abraham visited us in the U.S.

The meetings in the

windowless church building in Hyderabad were held with the traditional light that was used in those days. Since there was no electricity, kerosene lanterns were used. As the lanterns gave off a lot of heat along with the light, the already high temperature of the weather became exceedingly hot, but that could not dampen the sweet moving of the Spirit; many were filled, and even now I can visualize Philip Abraham and Phil dancing together for joy in the Spirit!

It was during one of these meetings that someone leaned over to tell me that a band of men were outside waiting to stone us. We had already been told that men had stoned the car of some missionaries who had come just a few months earlier, so immediately I understood the implication of their words. As I looked down at our baby in my arms, I wondered how he would survive a stoning. While considering these things, I felt a wave of peace sweep over me, and fear was gone. I knew that we were in God's hands. Phil, not knowing the situation, continued ministering to the sick and needy for an unusually long time that night; by the time we left the meeting, our would-be afflicters had gotten tired and gone away. We were sorry to learn that some of the believers who had left earlier had been beaten. That experience, along with some similar ones that happened later, led me to know that God is in control. I am not a brave person, but I feel that God is able to give us the grace we need in the time that we need it.

While still in Hyderabad we received word from the Jennings that they would be arriving by ship in Bombay (now known as Mumbai) in a few days. As Phil read the letter and began to consider the matter, he told me that he felt we should drive back to Bombay to meet them and help them get started in India. I explained to him that I didn't think this would be possible. This is why . . .

When we had originally driven over the road from Bombay to Hyderabad only three weeks earlier, we had only been able to go very slow—maybe 15 or 20 miles an hour. The unpaved road was like a washboard as we painfully went bump, bump, bumpity along. Every so often we would see a gypsy lady sitting alone (or with a baby) by the side of the road with a pile of rocks by her. These ladies

"For we walk by faith, not by sight"—2 Cor. 5:7

had been given the job of breaking up those large rocks into smaller rocks with the only tool that was given them—a hammer. We knew that eventually, when the stones had all been broken into the right size, some worker would load them into a small shallow basket which was shaped like a large dust pan. The worker would then place the basket on his head to carry the gravel to the right place to dump it onto the road. It would be a slow, laborious task. Since the only road machinery that we saw in India in those days was a small roller which had to be pulled by oxen, and the asphalt had to be melted and poured on the roads by hand, it was evident that paving a road would be a very slow process! Being pregnant, I just could not bear the thought of another arduous journey over that bumpy road—even if it was to pick up our best friends! Having fervently expressed my opinion to Phil, I waited for his answer. Phil, being a man of prayer, continued to seek for God's will. The answer seemed to be that we should return to Bombay to pick up the Jennings.

Chapter 18

Reunited with The Jennings

—Helen—

The day came for our trip to Bombay. What a wonderful surprise God had waiting for us! We were able to go full speed on that road, and it seemed as though we were being lifted up by the wings of angels. There was no natural explanation. It was impossible for the road to have been repaired. God was fulfilling His Word in Ps. 91:11–12: *"For he shall give his angels charge over you, to keep you in all your ways. In their hands they shall bear you up, lest you dash your foot against a stone."* (KJV). What a glorious trip it was!

Jonathan and Phillip Jennings

Our reunion with the Jennings was a joyous one, and our son Jonathan was happy to see his friend Philip. Even though our son had stood alone for the first time on the ship coming over to India, he had not taken his first step yet. Since Philip was already walking, it wasn't long before Jonathan started walking, too.

The Jennings had some interesting testimonies to recount while we spent a few days together in Bombay. It seems that they had arrived in England with almost no money. When the ship was met by immigration officials, the passenger in front of them was not allowed to get off of the ship, for he didn't have enough finances to sustain him in England. Then it was the Jennings' turn. As they stepped up in faith to the official, they explained that they were trusting God to supply their finances; even though they hardly had any money with them, they were allowed to get off the ship and fulfill their ministry in England.

When they had set sail from England for India, they had boarded a Polish vessel. Since Poland was under the control of Russia, they had been eating their meals right under a huge picture of Stalin that was hanging in the dining room; however, one day they saw that there was an announcement for a church service on the ship's bulletin board. Not realizing that it was the state church of Poland being announced, they took heart and asked for permission to have a service on the boat. Having received that permission, Dorothy went to work making a handout that had choruses on one side of the sheet of paper and scriptures on the other side. When she was about finished, she had one verse left over that wouldn't fit on the scripture side, so she just put it at the bottom of the chorus side. That verse was Romans 6:23. Much to her surprise, someone in the service asked to sing the chorus that was at the bottom of the page. Not wanting to disappoint the one who requested it, she stepped out in faith and began playing and singing, "For the wages of sin is death, but the gift of God is eternal life through Jesus Christ our Lord, through Jesus Christ our Lord." We have enjoyed singing that chorus ever after.

Since we were in Bombay, Phil asked another missionary if he knew any place that we could buy peanut butter. The next day a servant came bringing a 5-pound can of peanut butter as a gift from the missionary. In only a matter of a few days, the Jennings and we had devoured all of the contents; it tasted so-o good! We took the Jennings with us back to Hyderabad and enjoyed some time of ministering together.

One day Phil, Dorothy and Ray all went downtown, but I stayed behind to do some ironing. While Phil was away, he began to feel a strong urge to rebuke death in my behalf. Thankfully, he obeyed God; when he returned to where we were staying, he learned what had happened. We had brought a travel iron with us from the States. Since the electrical current in India is 230 volts, I needed to use an adapter plug for the iron. I, being completely ignorant of electrical matters, did a very foolish thing. When I finished ironing and was unable to pull out the adapter plug, I took a spoon in each hand and attempted to pry out the plug. Immediately I felt the electrical current flow up my arms and hit strongly with a bang on my upper forearms. At the same time, the current flowed down my upper body, but it abruptly stopped just as it was about to reach my womb where I was carrying our second child, Sarah. How we praised God together as we realized how God had protected me and our child by Phil's obedience and faithfulness to follow the urge of the Spirit to pray for me!

Cooking in India brought new experiences to me. We had taken a little Coleman camp stove with us, but we weren't able to use it long, for we had difficulty in obtaining the right fuel for it; however, it was a blessing for a time. The crows were easily enticed by the good smell of the food, so we were constantly trying to protect our meals from them, since there was no glass or screens on the windows to keep them out. We learned that we could buy something like Malt-o-meal, so we asked someone to buy some for us. When I started to cook it, I discovered that it was full of weevils. I mentioned this to the one who had purchased it, thinking she would exchange it for some that was good. Her response was, "Just heat it in a pan until the bugs die, then cook it and eat it." Another time I asked for some flour. While Phil and the Jennings were away for a while, I cooked some biscuits for them with the flour. They raved and raved about how delicious the biscuits tasted, but since I had spent about an hour picking ratted hair, bugs and other things out of the flour before I could cook with it, I couldn't even eat one of them! I thought it better not to tell them why I decided not to eat any biscuits.

Before long the Jennings and we decided that more could be accomplished if we went our separate ways, so they began going to some villages for meetings while we went to others. We didn't meet again until we had both returned to the States.

Chapter 19

What's It Like to Be in the Zoo

—Helen—

I remember so well some of the messages that Phil preached as we went to different places. One of his favorite subjects was in Galatians 5:19–25, regarding the works of the flesh and the fruit of the Spirit. Even though we were young and didn't know much, God began to move in a gracious way. We saw many saved, filled with the Spirit and healed. A number of supernatural healings took place as the people simply believed the Word.

Earlier I mentioned the challenge I had overcome when it came to "love feasts". I found the same challenge when it came to taking communion, for it was almost always served only using one cup for everyone. We often stayed in homes in the villages where the conditions were very unsanitary, but God was faithful to keep us from any serious sickness.

I had been raised by a mother who was very germ conscious. One of the things that made us want to pray harder about our health in some of the homes where we stayed was the sight of the dishes being washed. At the end of each meal, the dishes would be set outside for the dogs to lick; then the dishes would be scrubbed with the dirt outside in the same place where the dogs had been. Next they would be rinsed with water before being dried with a cloth that had been hanging over the person's shoulder. (That cloth was sometimes used as a handkerchief, too.) Finally, the plates and other dishes would be put on the shelf, ready to be used for the next meal.

One three-day trip especially stands out to us. We were invited to go to an island off the east coast of India. In order to ferry our car across, two narrow canoes were strapped together and some boards were laid crosswise on them so that we could drive the car on board. Upon our arrival we were brought something to drink. It was so dark that we couldn't tell by looking whether it was tea, coffee or something else. Upon inquiring about it, we found out that the water had come from a lake that we could see from where we were sitting. The lake was filled with people bathing, while others were washing their clothes or their animals in the water. For the first time, we felt that we couldn't even trust our water purifying tablets to make the liquid drinkable. Seeing our consternation, one of the believers quickly went out and shimmied up a coconut tree. Soon he was back with refreshing coconut water. This was our first introduction to the fizzy, clear-colored water that comes from a green coconut. After drinking the coconut water, the coconut was cracked open, and we ate the gelatin-like substance that was in the beginning stage of the formation of coconut meat inside the shell. The water and the gel were both so delicious! During our entire stay on that island, the only liquid we drank was coconut water.

Before our arrival on the island, the men had put up a small, one-room palm-leaf shack for us to sleep in, and they had dug a hole in the ground for our toilet. The toilet, too, was surrounded by palm branches. Since the people had never seen a white person before, they were very curious. Whenever we would be in our little sleeping shack, both men and children would simply part the leaves of the palm branches and have a look. We felt like monkeys in a zoo, for one time I counted at least ten or twelve faces that were staring at us at the same time through the holes they had made. It was easy for them to pull back the palm leaves so they could get a first-hand of view our activities without any hindrance. It was quite comical.

Besides these natural sidelines, there was some very blessed fruit from those meetings. A palm-leaf shelter had been constructed for the services. One night Phil was calling out various sicknesses by the word of knowledge and asking people to come forward for prayer, if they had that particular sickness. One time he called out that someone had stomach trouble, but no one responded. Even though the call was made more than once, the meeting was dismissed without anyone coming forward. It wasn't until after we had left that place that the pastor told us what had happened. There had been a Hindu priest who had been sitting in the shadows outside the shelter. He was the one with stomach trouble, but he was afraid of what people would think if he answered the call. After going home, he decided to put Jesus to the test. He asked God to heal him, if He was real. God healed him! The next morning he looked up the pastor and told him what had happened. The priest accepted Jesus as His Savior. The result was that all of the priest's family was saved, and the priest became a preacher of the gospel. Truthfully, often we never know the results of our labor; our responsibility is just to be faithful and leave the rest up to Him.

Chapter 20

Hot, Hotter, Hottest

—Helen—

The hottest season in India is between March and May. When the peak of the hot season was upon us, we arrived at Enid Morrison's home in Kakinada. Enid was a kind American missionary who had invited us to stay with her until the hot season was over. We were enjoying some special treats while we were with her, for she had a cook who knew how to cook Western style. The first few meals were almost heavenly in taste, but after a while we began to notice that we were being served the same meal every night. It was then that we learned that the cook had only learned how to make one Western-style meal, and the missionary had eaten that same meal every night for many years!

There are three seasons in India. Fortunately, we had arrived in India during the cool season. At that time the weather felt comfortable to us but cold to the Indians. This gave us the opportunity to slowly adjust to the warming temperatures before the real hot season took over. The cool season gave place to the dry season when there was no rain. As the dry weather continued, it got hotter and hotter until later when the rains came again. I like hot weather, but I have never been as hot as that time in India.

Remember how we said that God always gave us a shower of rain the night before we left on a trip, and then covered us with a cloud during the trip? I'll tell you about the one time that was different.

The night before we were scheduled to go to Rajahmundry to have special meetings, we were having a service outside in Enid Morrison's compound, and Phil was teaching on the gift of prophecy. In the service there was a young man who had recently become a Christian, and just that night he had prophesied for the first time. After the service he came to us with the word that he felt we shouldn't go on the trip the next morning. The missionary had agreed with him by saying, "It's just too hot to travel. Stay here until the weather gets cooler." It would take several hours to get to our destination, but we felt we must go, for there was no telephone service and we had no way of letting the pastor know of our change of plans; besides that, "the young man who had given us the prophetic warning had only prophesied for the first time the night before! Surely, he didn't yet know the mind of the Lord," we thought.

The next morning we set out on our journey. There was no rain, and no clouds appeared. It was extremely hot! When we finally arrived at the pastor's house, he told us that the meetings had been cancelled. There was nothing to do but to turn around and go back to the missionary's home in the hot, hot weather with no rain and no cloud covering. We learned once again that there is suffering when we move outside of God's will. God had tried to stop us and save us that journey, but we hadn't listened.

The Lord graciously continued healing people from various diseases and afflictions. It was a joy to see blind eyes see and deaf ears open. The six-and-a-half months we spent in India laid the foundations for our ministry. We made lifetime friends with the Indians, and we learned many valuable lessons. Now it was time to return to the States for more training in God's Bible school of practical experience, sometimes called "The School of Hard Knocks!"

It was a challenge to get our clothes dry enough to pack for the trip. As soon as I would get the clothes on the line, it would seem as though buckets of water would start pouring down. I would bring the clothes in until the downpour ceased, hang them out again, and here would come another downpour. The rainy season had begun.

Chapter 21

Homeward Bound

—Helen—

Finally we got packed in time to board an Italian luxury liner bound for Sri Lanka, and from there we boarded an English freighter. I was five and a half months pregnant. The ship made several stops, but we never left the ship during the 26 days that it took to sail to Boston. We could have gotten off in Egypt, but the Egyptians were shooting the British at the time, and we didn't want to run the risk of being shot.

During the trip home, we were in a storm and the waves were high. Even Phil was feeling seasick, but miraculously I didn't get seasick at that time. In fact, a song kept going over and over in my heart and on my tongue. It was

> *Fear thou not for I'll be with thee.*
> *I will still thy Pilot be.*
> *Never mind the tossing billows.*
> *Take My hand and trust in Me.*
>
> Course from hymn "I will pilot thee" by Mrs. Emily D. Wilson

It wasn't until we were back in our home church in Dallas some days later that we heard from our pastor's wife that she had been interceding for us just at the time of the storm, for she had felt that the ship was going to sink. Oftentimes we never know how God is working on our behalf because of the prayers of others.

There was another outstanding thing that took place on that trip. God told Phil that millions of people will be saved in the last days. Phil even saw God pointing to a map of Japan while stating that millions of people would be saved in Japan. To this day, Phil has continued believing and confessing that which God showed him then.

As we landed in Boston and boarded a taxi for the bus station, we felt like holding on for our dear lives. It seemed so strange to see all the traffic after being in India. We went from Boston to New York. After spending a day there, we boarded a bus for Waco, Texas, and were able to arrive in Waco just at the beginning of the semi-annual convention in October. We were both much thinner than when we had left, but we were safe and well. God had taken good care of us. When Phil's turn to preach came, his text was I Thessalonians 5:16–22:

> Rejoice ever more. Pray without ceasing. In everything give thanks: for this is the will of God in Christ Jesus concerning you. Quench not the Spirit. Despise not prophesyings. Prove all things; hold fast that which is good. Abstain from all appearance of evil.

Increase

By now the Jennings, too, had returned home; so we made plans to go to Overton, Texas, for a tent meeting in November. The weather was cold, but we had a big, pot-bellied wood stove in the tent. Conveniently, the time rolled around for our second child to be born while we were there, so we looked up the midwife that had delivered Jonathan. On November 22, Sarah Ruth came into the world. Mother and Dorothy were both with me once again. The Lord had given Phil and me the name Ruth long before our baby's birth; but we knew that was to be our daughter's middle name, not her first. It was several days later as I was looking at our little wrinkle-faced baby dressed in a blue gown that I realized that Sarah should be her first name. Sarah, which means "Princess," and Ruth, which means "Friendship," have proven to be prophetic in her life.

While traveling different places holding meetings, I became pregnant with our third child. Once again there was a decision to make. Where should this baby be born? Since we always stayed with Mother in Dallas in between meetings, it seemed logical to try to find a midwife in Dallas. I started making phone calls to different government and medical agencies. Each place would refer me to another place. Finally, I was able to get in contact with someone who knew about the midwives. I was informed that there were three in Dallas; however, as the person giving me information over the phone listed each one she would say, "But don't have this one; such and such is wrong with her! For sure don't have that one, because of this or that!" She never told me even one of their names, or how I could contact any of them. In those days, it was almost as if people thought you were signing your death warrant if you went to a midwife.

Phil and I decided to strike out on our own to find a midwife, so we went to the black section of Dallas and began asking people on the street. Occasionally someone would say, "Oh, I've heard that there is one somewhere," or "My sister-in-law used to be one," but we were never able get any information that would actually lead us to one. Finally, we decided to pack up and head for Overton once again. Now it was clearer to us than ever that God had supernaturally led us to the midwife in Overton when our first child had been born.

Expecting our baby to come a little early as usual, we rented a house for one month. That would give us two weeks to wait for the baby and two weeks for me to recover. This time Mother and Dorothy were not with us, so we were on our own. Two weeks went by, and we had no baby. As we were approaching the fourth week, we began getting concerned; so Phil and I set out for a long walk. That Saturday night I began feeling slight pains during the evening prayer meeting, but I thought we had plenty of time before the birth. However after going home, we decided Phil had better go for the midwife right away. It was a real blessing to me when I heard the squeal of our jeep as it rounded the corner by our house, for the midwife had barely stepped inside the door when I gave the final push and Rachel made her entry into this world. After bathing Rachel, the midwife told us she had increased her fee. However, since we had been such good customers, she would only charge us the same price she had charged the other two times. That price was just $25!

The Itch!

Now we had our family of three, and we were ready to continue our travels. Our trips took us to various places, but we were in and out of Arkansas from time to time. One time as I was sitting at the breakfast table in a house that had been provided for us during our stay, my ankle was itching, so I reached down to scratch it. Immediately I saw a big rat scurry away from under the table. Imagine our consternation when my ankle began itching again just a few minutes later, and once again a big rat scurried away when I reached down to scratch. Since Rachel was still a baby and was sleeping in a play pen just inches off the floor, we had a real prayer meeting each night before putting her to bed. The Lord answered our prayers, and no rat ever appeared again.

Chapter 22

What Did You Say, God?

—Helen—

Costa Deir

Five years into our full time ministry, we had a most unusual experience. As we were returning to Dallas after a ministry trip, I suddenly felt like the hand of God was pushing down on my head. I felt like God was telling me I would not be leaving Dallas again anytime soon. At the same time God was telling Phil that he was to stop traveling, and that he should get a job in Dallas. We had made the decision at the beginning of our ministry to be full-time laborers in the work of the Lord, so it seemed like a contrary thing God was telling us; but with both of us receiving the same message, we knew God was leading. Phil bought a newspaper and started perusing it for job openings. That turned out to be unnecessary, for God had already planned out everything. One day we went to the big farmer's market in Dallas. As we were preparing to leave, we met some missionary friends of ours whom we had last seen in India, where they had just finished holding large salvation and healing meetings. Now they had opened an office in Dallas, and they asked Phil to work for them. After prayer, Phil accepted.

Not long after starting to work in their office, a man named Costa Deir came from Ramallah, Jordan, to work in the same office. Costa had been rather newly filled with the Spirit, and he came to America hungry for more of God. As Phil and Costa worked together, Phil invited Costa to go with him to Waco. After several hindrances, the way was opened for us all to attend the semi-annual convention there. Pastor Glenn Ewing asked Costa to share his testimony. As he began to speak, many prophets from all over the building gathered around Costa and prophesied that God would use him as an apostle. After the service he asked what had happened, and Phil explained to him about personal prophecy. He was amazed and really wanted to know more.

As Phil and Costa continued working together, Costa fell in love with a precious girl named Ruth who was working in the same office. It wasn't long before Costa proposed to Ruth. Phil became the best man at their wedding; then, as suddenly as God showed Phil to start working, God told him to stop. Once again we were released to return to our traveling ministry. We then clearly understood that God's purpose for Phil's working that year in Dallas had been to spend time with Costa to get him introduced more into the moving of the Spirit. Later Costa became the mission director for Elim Bible Institute and God used him for many years to minister in many nations around the world.

Chapter 23

More Lessons Learned Off the Beaten Path

—Helen—

While the children were still young, we moved to Nebraska for a short season to take care of the church we had visited on our very first ministry trip. The pastor and his wife needed someone to watch over the church temporarily while they went to start another church. This was in 1958.

The town of Gering was off the beaten path. We were used to being around a lot of people, so it was a different experience for us. The church was above ground, and the living quarters were in the basement of the church. There was one big stove in the center of the basement to heat the whole downstairs. Since the congregation was small, so were the offerings; in fact, Phil began to realize that the average one was about $11 weekly. This was not much for a family of five to live on, so Phil decided he had better look for work. As he considered the matter though, God said, "No, just trust in Me." God wanted to show us more of His power, for He was preparing us for the days ahead. Phil

"For we walk by faith, not by sight"—2 Cor. 5:7 • **85**

felt impressed that we should begin writing our weekly needs on a piece of paper to present to the Lord. This included money for food, clothing, gasoline, utilities, bills, or whatever else was needed. We would then pray over the needs and wait for the answer. God was so faithful to give us everything we requested. Two special instances stand out in our minds.

Phil's father was now an evangelist, and we received word that he was coming to visit us. This was a very special occasion, for we rarely saw him. Wanting to prepare something special for our honored guest, I decided to make banana pudding for dessert. The only problem was that we didn't have money for the pudding or bananas. We made out our grocery list and prayed. When the day came for Phil's dad to arrive, everything we needed had come in except the bananas.

There was one thing that we always had plenty of, and that was vegetables—especially greens. The relative of someone in the church had planted a garden in the country and then moved away, so we were told we could go pick vegetables there any time we wanted. Phil went out to the garden that day; when he was getting ready to leave, the lady from the church handed him a paper sack. It was full of bananas! With great amazement Phil took the bananas and asked, "How did you happen to give us these bananas?" The lady answered, "My neighbor was out driving, and she came across a banana truck that had broken down. The driver, needing to get rid of the bananas quickly, was selling them at a very cheap price. The neighbor lady decided to buy several sacks to share with her neighbors. When she heard from the church lady that her pastor was coming out to get some vegetables, she handed our friend a sack saying, "Give this to your pastor." We never knew if the Lord had the truck break down in answer to our prayers, or what, but this one thing we knew: God had answered our prayer and we were filled with thanksgiving to God for His faithfulness!

We had tried to live as frugally as possible, believing that God was only interested in supplying our bare necessities, so we didn't ask God for anything special for ourselves. However, one day Phil felt that God would be pleased to give us more meat, so we decided to ask God for more. It just so happened that I had decided to keep a diary about that time. Amazingly, when I checked through my recordings at the end of a month, I discovered that the Lord had supplied thirty pounds of meat during that one month!

The time in Nebraska seemed to be lonely, and that feeling was amplified by the fact that all of our children had a bad case of the flu followed by whooping cough. This meant that I was unable to attend any of the church services for about two months. Fortunately, I could hear some of the music from above; however the main source of my comfort was found during the times I spent by the big black stove in the living room. It was there by the fire that I spent many a dark night praying as I was up taking care of the children during their sickness. The trial seemed long, but as I looked back later on that time, I realized that it was one of the most blessed times of my life. God was giving me a time to have fellowship with Him and Him alone. It was a time of quietness before the busy season ahead. It was as though the stove had become my altar.

The Dream

One night I had a dream that thirteen Indians appeared at our door. A few days later we were surprised by the unannounced arrival of the Jennings family and some others accompanying them. It was decided that we should have a convention. During those services our hearts were stirred and we felt it was time to leave once again for a mission field. The Jennings had ministered in Mexico and were planning on returning, so we packed up our things and followed them shortly thereafter. I then understood that the dream about the Indians meant that the Jennings were going to come bringing a missionary vision with them. We had spent five months in Gering and God had taught us many valuable lessons that would last a lifetime. He wanted us to know that He would meet our needs in any country of the world.

Chapter 24

Mexico

—Helen—

Looking back, it was humorous that we traveled to Mexico. Mother had always been interested in Spanish, and I had had some interest, too. When I was around fourteen or fifteen years old, the opportunity arose for me to study a little with a missionary who was home from Peru, and I readily accepted. I was surprised one day though, when she gave me homework to compose a gospel message in Spanish. I thought laughingly in my heart, "She thinks I'm going to be a missionary to Spanish-speaking people. Ha, ha, ha! I will never go to minister where I will need Spanish!" You see, I had India on my heart. I found out later that God was preparing me for the future, for Spanish-speaking countries would be very much a part of my life in the days to come.

Those first trips in and out of Mexico were filled with joys and sorrows. It was such a blessing to minister to hungry, receptive hearts, and we loved it. The unlovely part included diarrhea, bed bugs, mosquitoes, and stones. As I washed Rachel's diapers and spread them out on the bushes, the mosquitoes were always waiting to bite. Those were days of real persecution in Mexico. One time we were staying in the back of a building where we were holding meetings. Dorothy had laid her youngest child on a bed to sleep during service, and as an afterthought, she decided to let down a mosquito net over the child. During the service we could hear stones being thrown on the building. When we returned to our rooms after the service ended, we discovered that a rock was on the mosquito net just above the child's head. It was only the mosquito net that had kept the child from being hit.

It could be very dangerous to pass out tracts in some of the fanatical places, but we learned about a special method to use for distributing literature. As we drove along, when we saw someone we would roll up a tract in a small square of brightly colored cellophane and throw it out the window. We would even throw out bunches of them as we were about to leave a city. When we turned around to look, we could  see people scrambling to pick up those messages of hope. Reading material was scarce for many in those days, and the colorful little cylinder-shaped things, barely bigger than a cigarette, stirred up curiosity. Our prayer was that many would be reached for Christ as they read. It has been a blessing in recent years to know that there are churches in some of those same places that we passed through.

As we drove from village to village, our hearts would be so touched, for in many places there were no telephones with which to notify people of our coming. Even if we arrived somewhere in the evening, someone would set out with a lantern in hand to walk by night to another village to announce the coming services. The people would come by foot, or by whatever means they could find to attend the meetings, and the Lord would mercifully save, fill, and heal the people.

It was our custom to stay with the people in their homes, often sleeping on the dirt floor inside or outside the adobe house. At times we would even be sleeping on the floor with the whole family that lived in the house. Our son Jonathan and the Jennings' son Philip were the best of friends. One day they were having a good time playing with their little cars inside the adobe house where we were staying, and we noticed that they had made a road for their cars. As our eyes followed the direction of the road, we were horrified to see that they had innocently made a tunnel for their cars . . . right through the adobe wall of the house!

On one trip we had services in a village at the foot of Mt. Orizaba. The pastor there had a big long scar on his face, for he had been a very rough sinner in his day. In fact, he told us that he used to take a gun and shoot at his wife's feet, so that he could make her dance. God had transformed him into a very gentle man. Every morning when we went outside to eat breakfast under a tree, there would be a bucket of water so we could wash our hands, and floating in the water would be a beautiful flower that had been placed there by that man's loving hands.

From the church at the foot of the mountain, we went to a church that was halfway up Mt. Orizaba. As we were making our way up the mountain, the believers were coming down to meet us with garlands of flowers, and the songs of joy and praise they were singing to the Lord were being wafted along through the air. When we reached the church, it was full of flowers and fragrance. This whole scene was made more precious to us as we listened to the history of that

Mt. Orizaba is the highest mountain in Mexico and the third highest in North America. Wikipedia

church, and of another that was at the top of the mountain. Many years earlier in the midst of severe persecution, the believers in that area had been tied to horses and dragged down the mountain. Now along that same pathway where the believers had been dragged, praises to God were ringing out. We had gone to the church on the bottom and the one halfway up, but we weren't able to go to the one on top. We heard that it was very cold, and the people living there were very poor and had little with which to cover themselves.

In many of the villages where we went, the pastor would have us all stand in a circle after the meeting was over on the last night. While we were all holding hands, we would sing an old chorus with many tears running down our faces. "'Til we meet, 'til we meet, 'til we meet at Jesus' feet. 'Til we meet, 'til we meet. God be with you 'til we meet again." How much we appreciated those parting blessings in song, because to my knowledge, we have never had the opportunity to meet them again on this earth. There will be a joyous reunion in Heaven one day!

Miraculous Answer to Prayer

We were in and out of Mexico and Central America for the next few years. After one of those early trips I found myself unable to swallow regular food when we arrived home. Even though the people with whom we stayed in Mexico always gave us the best that they had, often even sacrificing greatly to do so, we had been sustained with a mostly liquid diet of soup, greens, tea, etc. The normal food we eat in the States felt so dry and heavy that my mouth and stomach wouldn't accept it until I had spent a few days gradually getting readjusted to the diet. We don't know how blessed we are with such plenty here in our homeland. Because of this experience, and our sometimes severe bouts with diarrhea, we had a prayer request that was miraculously answered a short time later.

The Jennings were with us in Houston, Texas, having meetings at a church pastored by Joe Tilata. When we were about to return yet again to Mexico, we asked Pastor Tilata to pray for us that God would adjust our stomachs in such a way that we would be able to digest the food and fare well with whatever God gave us to eat. Well, Pastor Tilata didn't pray the way we asked him to pray. His prayer was, "God, please give them good food wherever they go." Do you know that no matter what country we have been in or how poor the people were, we have never had anything but good food from that day until this, and we have suffered only rarely from diarrhea! God truly answered his prayer!

A Test

Because religious fanatics were more apt to try to do harm on the last night of a meeting, we would usually leave town one day earlier than was announced. However, in one place where we had a meeting, someone came during the night and broke out the windshield of the Jennings' car, even though both cars were parked right in front of where we were sleeping. Ray, knowing that it would not be possible to continue driving through Mexico with the broken windshield, began making plans to return to the States, but none of us had money for the trip. We spent a few days with Pastor Miguel Flores before leaving, while believing God to supply what was needed. One morning we noticed that breakfast was later than usual. After it arrived, Pastor Flores told us that he hadn't had money for breakfast that morning; but as he was praying, a man arrived with some money. God had been speaking to the man that morning to take the Flores family some money, but the man had said to God, "They don't need any money; they have those rich Americans staying with them." God has ways of convincing people of His will. After a short time of arguing with God, the man had begun feeling like he was having a problem with his heart. He ended up coming to Pastor Flores for prayer; in the process, he gave the pastor the money that God had told him to give. The needs were met both for the pastor and his family, and for us. We had a delicious breakfast that day, and soon we had the money to drive back to the States.

In the olden days, churches sometimes gave the evangelist what they would call a "pounding". That meant that the people would bring gifts of food for the evangelist. When we were in one church in south Texas, the pastor's wife announced that they would have a "pounding" for us. The people brought so many canned goods and things that as we were packing our car full, I felt like we had almost been pounded to death. Little did I know that the food that was given to us then would have to last for many a day, because there was a long space ahead when we had no meetings. It made me think of the scripture about Elijah in 1 Kings 19:5–8:

> *Then as he lay and slept under a broom tree, suddenly an angel touched him, and said to him, "Arise and eat." Then he looked, and, behold, there by his head was a cake baked on coals, and a jar of water. So he ate and drank, and lay down again. And the angel*

of the LORD came back the second time, and touched him, and said, "Arise and eat; because the journey is too great for you." So he arose, and ate and drank, and he went in the strength of that food forty days and forty nights as far as Horeb the mountain of God.

I adopted a motto when we were in the evangelistic field: "Eat as much as you want at each meal, for you never know when your next meal will be." It really wasn't that God ever let us go without food, but sometimes meal schedules varied greatly! Also, we found at times we would have watermelon, watermelon and more watermelon—or chicken, chicken and more chicken. Then for a long time we wouldn't have any watermelon or chicken. We just learned to be thankful for what we had when we had it!

Chapter 25

The Unplanned Stop

—Helen—

Once again we found ourselves in Hot Springs—this time at a church pastored by Bob Boyles and his wife Mary. The Ernest McCarty Family had gone from that church to Honduras as missionaries, and we were planning on driving down to Honduras with the Jennings to minister and to spend some time with them. It would prove to be an eventful trip.

The Lord graciously provided us with a beautiful panel truck, and a brother in the church offered to make the payments on it for us. The Jennings already had a car. The people in the church donated many canned goods that they thought would be a blessing to the missionaries; so we loaded them in the panel truck along with shovels, in case we had trouble on the highway and had to dig ourselves out. (The Pan American Highway on which we were to travel was still under construction.) We took some folding cots, too, so we would have a place to sleep.

 We drove through Mexico without too much trouble, but things changed when we entered Guatemala. We were going over steep mountain roads at night, and the fog was hanging heavy over the road. Ascending an unusually steep pass, we saw a bus stopped on the side of the road. One tire had slipped off the highway, causing the bus to hang precipitously over a cliff. People were standing all around. It would have been impossible to start the climb again from where we were if we had stopped, so we had to just keep on going, even though we would have liked to help.

Along the way, the Jennings' car started having trouble, but the Lord helped it to limp along until we reached Guatemala City. We knew we could go no farther without getting it fixed. We had stopped in Cuernavaca, Mexico, and someone there had given us the phone numbers for two people they knew in Guatemala City, but there was no answer at either place. As we were praying and wondering what to do, we saw a man on a street corner. The man told us to go to the church he attended, and he gave us directions.

We soon arrived at the church and met the pastor. He had never heard of us, but he graciously offered to let us set up our cots in the church. He and his wife even invited us to eat with them. We spent several days there waiting to get our car fixed. Meanwhile the pastor, Fernando Reyes, was observing us. It seems that we passed the test, for he asked us to have some special meetings—thus, the revival began. We had services every night for ten days, and the Lord filled seventy people with the Holy Spirit. It was a glorious time! As it turned out, this unplanned stop in Guatemala turned out to be the highlight of our whole Central American trip, and a relationship was formed that lasted until Brother Reyes went to be with the Lord many years later.

Philip, Pastor Fernando Reyes & Ray Jennings

We certainly never know how God will lead and what circumstances He will arrange to direct us in His paths. Even though we were at that church for over two weeks that time, and then several times later over the years, we never again saw the man who had been standing on the street corner when he directed us to "his home church." We have often wondered, "Was he one of the angels whom God sends to minister to His people?"

Honduras

We arrived in Honduras and rented a place in the annex of a hotel for a while before going further. It was used as a storage place, and we would sit at our table and watch the big rats run around in the rafters while we were eating. One time I tried to step on a huge rat, but I just got his tail. When he flipped around and tried to bite me, I let him go in a hurry! When we first arrived, we were exceedingly thirsty; but we had no purified water. It was there that we learned what water purified with a little bleach tasted like! (Not the best, but it had to do for a while!) There was a young bull fighter staying at the annex to whom we had a chance to witness. I am still touched as I think of the sadness of the words he spoke: "After every bull fight I call my mother to assure her that I am still alive." We never heard more about him after that; I pray that he accepted the Lord as his Savior.

After a time we went on to Jutigalpa where the McCartys lived, and we happily presented all of the canned goods to them. To our surprise, it wasn't the blessing that we thought it would be, for the only means they had for the disposing of the trash was to throw it out the window onto the vacant lot next door. Every can that was thrown out would be soon collected by the natives. It was a rare thing for them to have a can, and they could find many ways to use such a precious commodity! This caused the McCartys concern, for it made them appear very rich to the natives, and they didn't want to make the natives feel they were different from them. I guess we live and learn both by our accomplishments and by our mistakes.

The McCartys had a van and a kerosene lantern that they would use for special meetings. The van had a big open space in the middle where all the children would sit or stand. One night after the meetings, Ernest put out the light and set the hot lantern in the car. Rachel, who was about three at the time, got her leg against the lantern and received a very bad burn. For days we would carry her and pray for her, but at last her leg healed. It was there, too, that Sarah became very sick with dysentery, and she would have to be carried out to the bush (which was the only bathroom), for she had no strength to walk on her own.

Even though there were various trials of sickness, the Lord brought us through them all as we prayed and looked to God for His help. While we were joyfully enjoying the ministry in Honduras, we received word from home that my mother greatly needed our help. It seemed necessary for us to return home at once, but that was the last thing we desired to do, and it brought tears to my eyes and pain to my heart. In fact, I just didn't have peace until Earnest McCarty handed me a prophetic poem that God had given him for me. I still carry that poem with me, for it truly ministered to my need.

> *As you travel from country to country,*
> *With no place to call your home*
> *Never able to say, "This is mine;*
> *I'll fix it up and be at home."*
> *Living with just God's Provision.*
> *Never knowing what tomorrow may hold;*
> *By the world you're despised and rejected,*
> *But you've got something better than gold.*
>
> *While the world is so anxiously struggling,*
> *To hoard up earth's treasures down here,*
> *While their hearts, nerves, and bodies are failing*
> *Filled with problems, worries and fears,*
> *You can travel along with a song in your heart,*
> *Not a worry to bother your mind;*
> *For the treasure you hold—it is worth more than gold,*
> *The Treasure? God's presence divine.*
>
> *To those who believe you are bringing*
> *Salvation, Deliverance from sin.*
> *To those burdened down with their sorrows,*
> *The message of sweet peace within.*
> *The dumb now can talk. Just believing*
> *Has broken the fetters, set them free.*
> *The blind see, the lame walk,*
> *Yes, God's message you've brought*
> *Yes, you carry Heaven's Treasures you see."*
>   —Earnest McCarthy, 1958

Rachel's leg was still recovering from the burn when we left Honduras, and I began feeling quite sick on the way. I had eaten a Popsicle from a street vendor before leaving Honduras, and by the time we reached Guatemala, I had turned quite yellow. The Jennings decided to sell their car in Guatemala and fly home; Dorothy was pregnant and Ray didn't feel that she was up to the drive home. It took some days for them to find the right buyer. In the process, Phil decided to sell our car, too. This proved to be a serious mistake. As always, whenever we would miss the will of God, a time of suffering would follow. When we arrived back at my Mother's in Dallas, Texas, I was beginning to feel better and Phil went out to look for a car with the money he had gotten from the sale of the beautiful panel truck that God had so graciously provided for us before we left for Honduras. The money wasn't enough to buy much, so we ended up with an ugly bright orange station wagon that had been used by the city. Besides being noisy and cold, it had a hole in the floor and in general was nothing but a wreck!

As we continued trying to follow God's plan for our lives, we would travel from place to place as the doors would open. Many times the special meetings would last for several days, a week, or even longer, but we would always plan to be in Waco, Texas, at the semi-annual conventions at Grace Gospel Church. Those were times of great refreshing for us, and we made many lasting friendships. The ones who attended became like family to us, and Mom and Dad Ewing were spiritual parents to us and to many a young preacher. Their arms were always open to receive us and give us what spiritual encouragement they could. Often before we would leave, we would feel cash being slipped into our hand when our hands would touch theirs. There was no charge for the conventions, meals or a place to stay. We spent many a happy time on the lumpy beds or cots located in a cabin, or in dormitories in the back of the church. The recipe for the delicious, eggless whole wheat pancakes that were served each morning during the convention is still one of our favorites. An offering was never "taken" in a church service or in the conventions, but the needs were always met as people placed their offerings in the little wooden box in the back of the church. Waco was not just a place to go for conventions, but it was a place to stop anytime you were passing through that way. There was daily morning prayer and teaching, along with the usual Sunday and weeknight services. Since

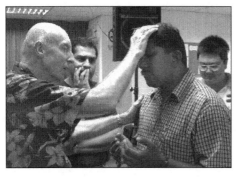

the Lord has used Phil in the prophetic word, and we have seen many people filled with the Spirit, we still come in contact with those who encourage us by telling us how the Lord used Phil to minister to them in those early days.

The Jennings had the baby they were expecting, so now they had a boy and two girls. So did we, and we were ready to start off on another trip together. They had made one trip to Hawaii previously and were making plans to go again. Ever since Phil had received his call to Japan, we had been holding it up to God about when we should go. It was decided that we would go to Hawaii with the Jennings and then on to Japan as missionaries. Before leaving, though, we made another trip together to Hot Springs, Arkansas. We were able to attend the wedding of two young people whom we loved dearly—Ken Horner (whom God had used to provide us a big duck for Thanksgiving when we had prayed for more meat in Nebraska) and Naomi Hooper. Since the Jennings and we were getting ready to leave for Hawaii, the church prayed for us. Pastor Boyle's mother-in-law shared something she saw during that prayer. She saw a ship leaving land and then turning around and coming back again. At the time we didn't realize how prophetic that was.

If we felt that God was leading us, it wasn't unusual for us to go ahead and make plans to go somewhere, even if we didn't have the money. We felt that it was our responsibility to find God's will. If we found it and obeyed it, we believed God would keep His part by paying for whatever He told us to do. Now we were about to put that principle to a greater test than ever before. Our whole trip to Hawaii was to be one big lesson in trusting God for our finances, and in His wisdom, God planned to give us a final exam at the end.

Chapter 26

The Land of Leis

—Helen—

Sometime earlier a young couple named Mel and Doris Amrine had loaded up their car and headed to Fuller Theological Seminary. Since they had heard about Grace Gospel Church in Waco, they decided to stop for a visit on their way. That short stop turned into a year or more that they spent at Grace Gospel Church. After having drunk in much ministry and teaching, they felt led to go to Honolulu, Hawaii, to start a work, so they sold all that they had and started out by faith for Hawaii in June of 1958. They began having meetings at Likiliki School in Honolulu. In time the group became Grace Bible Church. Hawaii was still a territory. All the ladies wore muumuus (long, loose flowery dresses), flip-flops were the fashion, and exotic flowers were everywhere. Leis were in abundance.

Amrines (Upper Middle) with Grace Bible believers

A few months after the Amrines started the work in Hawaii, the Jennings and we felt like the Lord wanted us to go to Hawaii, too. We wanted to strengthen them in the work as well as minister in the other islands before going on to Japan. The Lord graciously provided the plane fare and a few extra dollars. Mel met us at the airport, but he didn't have a car. In order to get Mel and the ten of us with all of our luggage to the Amrines' house, we needed two taxis. When we all pooled our money together, we had just enough to pay both taxi fares. At last we had arrived at our destination. It was so good to be together again with our friends, and our children were happy to have the Amrine's only child Laurie as their new playmate!

Ray and Dorothy were up and ready the next morning to visit a Japanese pastor whom they had met on their previous trip. Phil joined them, and I was left to watch all the children. The group returned later bubbling over with joy—the pastor had a Buick for us to use while we were in Hawaii. The only problem was that the battery was dead, so Phil and Ray had left the battery at a service station and said they would pick it up the next day. Of course, this was all by faith, for they had no money; however since I had received $35 in the mail while they were out visiting, I joyfully announced, "We have the money to pay for it!" That was our introduction into Hawaii, but there were many more good things to come.

We traveled to several of the islands, taking the car with us by ferry. One pastor on the big island of Hawaii was warned not to have the Jennings and the Stanleys come to his place lest he go broke caring for all of us. The pastor invited us to come anyway. Soon after the meetings started, the cook from the largest cattle ranch in Hawaii (Parker Cattle Ranch) came and was filled with the Spirit. He began to bring all kinds of food to the pastor. This included a case of canned milk (I loved to drink canned milk straight from the can) and great big quarters of beef. There was so much meat that we had to even eat meat for breakfast to keep it from spoiling. The pastor had never had so much meat in his life!

Another Filipino man invited us to his place. He said, "I don't have anything to offer you to eat except sweet potato vines, and I don't have a church. I just have Sunday School for children." We accepted his invitation by faith. Just before we left to go to his home, the man's overseer gave him a big sack of rice. Upon arriving at his house, we saw that the only food he had in his house was about ten or twelve small cans on his shelf, for he was a bachelor. His unbe-

lieving neighbors began bringing things to eat, among which were several large breadfruit.*

I had never seen breadfruit before, but we began experimenting with it. We boiled breadfruit, fried breadfruit, mashed breadfruit, and fixed it any other way we could think of. Not having had any experience with sweet potato vines, I remember that I overcooked them until they were mushy, but I did the best I knew how.

Among the delicacies we received from people was tripe (the stomach of a cow). We had never even heard of such a thing, but since it was God's provision we boiled it and did our best to eat it. Since it looked and tasted awful, none of us were happy to see that we had a good amount left over after we finished eating. Not ever willing to waste anything, we reluctantly put it aside for the next day's main meal. Before the next day arrived, however, we had an unexpected visit from some missionaries who lived in another town. We had never met them before, but we had a good time of fellowship together. As they were about to leave, I had a bright idea. "Do you like tripe?" I hopefully asked. "Oh, yes," they enthusiastically answered; "it is one of our favorite dishes." With a heart full of thanksgiving (that we wouldn't have to eat it again), I graciously gave them all that was left! To top it off, they explained that they didn't have any food to eat in their house, so it was truly a blessing to them.

One day as Phil and Ray arrived at a country store, they were amazed to see a missionary couple there whom we had briefly met several years earlier when we had first arrived in India. They had been leaving India just when we were arriving, but because they had missed their boat, it had been necessary for them to stay in India a few extra days. For that reason, we had been able to meet them before they left. After some happy greetings, the missionaries asked Phil about our son Jonathan's health. When Phil said that he was fine, they asked to see him. Thus it was that Phil and Ray showed up unexpectedly with those missionaries at the place we were staying,

---

Breadfruit grows on tall, beautiful trees. The fruit itself can sometimes grow to twelve inches in length and weigh up to thirteen pounds. It is very nutritious.

only to find Jonathan and Philip covered with dirt and happily playing. Then the missionaries told us how they had prayed much for Jonathan's health when they had seen us arrive in India with our baby, for they knew how disease-ridden India was. They were delighted to see how God had answered their prayer in keeping him well. This made us more thankful than ever for the good health we had enjoyed on our first missionary journey!

We were invited to minister on the small island of Molokai. Before leaving for Hawaii, we had purchased a portable battery-operated P.A. system, which consisted of a microphone on one end of a wire with the speaker on the other end. Phil and Ray decided to advertise the meetings by marching up and down the two-block downtown area of the town of Kaunakakai. The next day we were having a morning prayer meeting next to a large Catholic church. The children were outside playing. I thought perhaps I should check on them. To my astonishment (and embarrassment) I saw Jonathan and Philip imitating what their fathers had done the day before, but this time they were marching up and down in front of the Catholic church announcing the meetings in a loud voice saying, "Everyone is welcome; the chief priests, the high priests and the Catholic Priests!" At that point, I felt that it was best to bring the boys inside.

The outstanding event of that meeting was when a Salvation Army Captain came up for prayer. When Phil and Ray started praying for him, he suddenly fell backward on the concrete floor with a bang and began speaking in tongues; we were quite concerned about his welfare until he arose a short time later with a smile on his face and declared that he was perfectly well and hadn't been hurt at all in the fall!

The Exam

Phil and I had left home with the full intention of going on to Japan. As the time passed, though, we began feeling that we should return home. In fact, the Jennings and we all felt that God wanted us to be in Waco for the upcoming convention. There wasn't enough time to allow us to contact many people about our new plans, so we knew it would take a miracle for us to have enough money to go.

In those days you could reserve a plane ticket by just paying a ten percent deposit; the rest would be paid at the airport when you were ready to leave. We reserved tickets for Sunday afternoon and paid the down payment, but we didn't have enough money to fully pay for the tickets. We were earnestly praying and believing that God would supply the money.

Grace Bible Church had been our base while in Hawaii. We had enjoyed the teaching and fellowship of Mel and Doris Amrine, and our desire had been to contribute whatever we could to strengthen them and the church, so we were often in the services there. This particular Sunday morning was a time for us to say goodbye to all our friends. After the service was over and the people were gone, we saw that we still lacked a good amount of money. It was then that Mel told us about someone not long before who had said that they felt led to go home. That person had told the people that God was going to supply for him; but when the money didn't come in, it had been a stumbling block to the people. We certainly didn't want to be a bad example!

I'm sure that a good number of people would have gone to the airport to bid us goodbye, but our flight was delayed twice. The second delay meant that the plane would be leaving late at night, so we ended up putting all six children to bed. Then came the time of decision; what should we do?

Ray, Dorothy, Phil and I got down on our knees to pray. Should we really get the children up out of bed and go to the airport in the middle of the night when we didn't have the money for the tickets? It seemed that the other three felt we should go; in fact, Dorothy joyfully shouted, "Let's go!" like it was some great adventure. I can't say that I was quite so excited, but I agreed to go.

As we arrived at the airport with all our luggage, the man at the ticket counter came over to check us in. Phil said, "Wait just a minute."

While we had been in Hawaii, we had met a precious missionary. She was planning on going home to the Mainland the same time as we were, so we had invited her to go with us to the convention in Waco, for we thought it would be a blessing to her. She was the only person at the airport when we went, except for Mel and another lady. As she saw us praying, she came over and asked if we had the money for our tickets. Phil answered, "No, we don't." "How much do you need?" she asked. "Two hundred and thirty-nine dollars,"

Phil replied. She disappeared into the bathroom briefly. When she returned, she handed us the money.

She later told us she had received that money about two weeks earlier and had tried to put it into the bank right away. However, God wouldn't let her deposit it at that time. He was keeping the money for us.

With joy and thanksgiving, we all boarded the plane for Los Angeles. God had answered our prayers, and we had passed what seemed to be a final exam in trusting God for finances. It has never been quite so hard since then!

Our next problem was, "How are we going to get ourselves and our missionary friend to Waco, Texas in time for the convention?"

Chapter 27

Waco or Bust!

—Helen—

After arriving in Los Angeles, we all went to our friends' home in San Fernando Valley to prepare for our trip to Waco. There at John Myers's home, we found a letter from my mother with thirty-five dollars in it. How we praised God for this provision!

Soon after our arrival, a man arrived at John's house from Seattle. He was hoping to catch a ride to the Waco convention with the Myers, because he didn't have enough money to drive his own car all the way there and back home again. Seeing our predicament he said to us, "You can use my car to drive to Waco, if you have money to pay for the gas."

Full of enthusiasm and expectancy, we all piled into the car and began our journey. Our goal was to be in Waco for the opening service on Wednesday evening; however, we decided to stop and rest a few hours at a friend's house in Arizona. (In those days, it wasn't unusual for someone who was traveling to arrive unexpectedly at a friend's house anytime, day or night; often special meetings would then begin if the person who arrived was a preacher.)

During our time of rest, a Mexican arrived at our friend's home. He had hitchhiked from Mexico to see if he could catch a ride to the convention. We added him to the five adults and six children who were already in the car and continued our journey. We stopped only long enough to buy gas, milk and dates along the way. Miraculously, the thirty-five dollars that mother had sent paid for everything, and we arrived just in time for the first service in Waco! But that wasn't the end of God's provision. After the convention was over, the Jennings and we all drove away in a car. The man who loaned us the car gave it to the Jennings, and Costa Deir gave us a car. God had done exceedingly and abundantly above all that we could even ask or think!

God was mindful of our children, too. Shortly before we were to leave Hawaii, someone had given the children a lot of very nice toys, but it was impossible for us to bring all the toys on the plane. Each child had been able to choose one favorite toy, but the rest we had given away. One night during the convention, one of the ladies brought a big sack of dolls, doll clothes and other things to give the children.

Truly, Sister Denton's prophetic vision that she had shared with us in Hot Springs just before we left for Hawaii had been fulfilled. We thought we were on our way to Japan, but she had seen the ship leaving the U.S. and then coming back again. It was not yet God's time for us to go to Japan.

Even though the Jennings and we went our own ways for a little while after leaving Waco, it wasn't long before we were together again.

Phil and Ray in Taiwan with Steven Chin Jew
Ray is holding the banner on the left. Steven is next to the sign on the right.

Chapter 28

God Provides Again

—Helen—

We continued making trips in the States, Mexico and Guatemala. We would often stop in Pharr, Texas, on our way to and from Mexico. There was a huge room with a kitchen behind the sanctuary of the church in Pharr, where we all would stay. On one trip we discovered that the big sign that had been in the sanctuary had been moved to the room where we stayed. Even though Ray, Dorothy, Phil and I got along unusually well together, there would be occasional small conflicts that would arise. That sign that stretched across much of the back wall of our quarters was a good reminder to keep us in line.

> **That they all may be one.**
> John 17:21

In 1962, we spent a few months with our friends, the Brymers and the Henrys, in Cuernavaca, Mexico. Loretta Brymer and I took turns homeschooling Philip Jennings, Danny Brymer, and our son Jonathan. One morning all the children were at the Henrys' home eating some nice whole wheat hotcakes that Dorothy Henry was cooking, and I was doing the serving. The hotcakes were very delicious, so I think Jonathan had already downed about ten little ones when I went back into the kitchen to get some more on the serving plate. The large griddle had a number of them cooking on it. As I looked at the hot cakes, I noticed that many little heads were sticking up out of each one of them. Worms! It seems that Dorothy was down to the bottom of a big sack of flour, and she didn't realize that the flour was full of worms. It was really a funny sight to see, and we laughed to think that our children had had meat with their hotcakes that day!

After traveling here and there for the first ten years of our marriage, the thought of a home sounded really appealing. Phil, Ray and Doyle Brymer were going to make a trip together to Guatemala, and Phil and Ray wanted Dorothy and I to stay close to a good church at the border while they were away. Pharr seemed to be the logical place for us to stay. Our good friends Creed and Irene Davis pastored there. The Jennings found a small trailer house (as they were called in those days) to buy, so Dorothy and the children would have a place to stay. That made us think, "We need one, too; but where will the money come from?" We were used to living with just enough to get by and trusting God for every bite we ate, so this was a real challenge to our faith; but we began petitioning God the best we knew how.

Phil, Doyle, and Ray

Shortly before time for the Guatemala trip, we were once again at our friend's home in San Fernando Valley. While there, we received a special delivery letter with a check in it. Phil opened the letter, looked at the check, and said, "We have fifty dollars!" We gave thanks to God for His supply, but then Phil decided to look at the check once again. "It's FIVE HUNDRED DOLLARS!" he exclaimed. "It's the biggest check we've ever had!"

Our last trip before the men left for Guatemala was to Hot Springs, Arkansas again. As we left Hot Springs and were driving down the highway south toward Dallas, a sign in a trailer court caught our eye: "FOR SALE." "We don't have much money," we said, "but let's stop anyway and just inquire." A kind, elderly man met us at the door of the house trailer. "How much are you asking for your trailer," we asked? "Seven hundred dollars," he answered. "What? That's too good to be true," we thought. We had five hundred dollars. All we needed was two hundred more. Of course, it could have been two thousand as far as our financial condition was concerned. After consultation with each other and the Lord, we finally decided to call

Dad to see if he would be willing to loan us two hundred dollars. This was totally against what we had ever done before, because we really didn't believe in borrowing money; but as we thought about it, we decided to do it just this once. I called Dad, and he ended up giving us the money instead of loaning it. How blessed we were!

The owner of the trailer explained that he needed to go into a retirement place. Since he loved his trailer very much and hated to see it go, he made the price cheap so that he could sell it very quickly. He even left some nice pans and things in the trailer for us to keep. We thankfully bought the trailer, hooked it to our car then and there, and drove straight to Pharr, only stopping one night in Dallas on the way. The Jennings and we got set up in a trailer park, and Phil was only able to spend one night in the trailer before he left for Guatemala.

In the back of the twenty-three-foot trailer, we replaced the twin bed with a bunk bed. This made room for Sarah and Rachel to sleep on the bottom while Jon had the bed on the top. The breakfast nook made into a bed for Phil and me. There was only one small closet, but there were five little drawers—one for each of us; what fun it was to have a home of my very own! One time someone gave me a chicken, so I immediately invited company over to eat. I wanted someone to share the special meal with us.

It had been no surprise to me that we had not yet had a place of our own all of those ten years. True, in between meetings we could always go to Mother's and stay in what used to be my bedroom; but I had longed for a place I could call mine. Before we were married I often found myself singing the chorus of the song "My Home, Sweet Home" by Rev. N. B. Vandall. The words came from my heart, not my mind. The chorus talks of the Heavenly home that is waiting for us—our true home! I knew not to expect a natural home here on earth, and I had made that consecration ahead of time; however, I was very thankful to now have a place I could really call home!

When the men folk returned from a blessed seven-week revival in Guatemala City with Pastor Fernando Reyes, they had some interesting testimonies to share. One of the testimonies was how God had healed an elderly man who was about to die. His son had already built a coffin for his father. Phil came home with a picture of the healed man standing by the coffin he no longer needed.

It was time for the Jennings and us to pull our trailers to our next places of ministry, which turned out to be Mississippi and Alabama. We met the Pruitt family in Indianola, Mississippi, and we enjoyed working together with them for a while. Joe Lehman joined us for a time while we were there.

After less than a year of trailer life, God led us to Waco. It was there that we decided to rent our first house, which turned out to be a little three-room square house. We parked our trailer at the side of the house and were blessed by having a young couple named Dale and Thresa Barnes live in it. The Jennings rented a house down the street that was a little bigger than ours. I was very happy in our home, but when the Jennings decided to leave Waco some months later, we rented their house. Now I really felt like I was in Heaven. I was in a real house with real furniture. It didn't matter that the furniture was old and dumpy-looking—it was mine!

The rent for the house was twenty-seven dollars a month—a fortune for us. The landlady lived next door. She knew that we were in the ministry and only lived from day to day. Whenever I would go over to pay the rent each month, she would sometimes say, "I'm sorry to take this from you." My heart would respond by thinking, "You just don't know how thankful I am to have this money to pay," for sometimes the rent money would only come at the last minute!

That year in Waco turned out to be the first and last year that the children attended public school; up to that point, I had been teaching them. Jon was in the fourth grade, Sarah in the third and Rachel in the second.

One day Phil decided he would make a trip to Los Angeles. Now there were always two places that we never wanted to go, and those places were New York and Los Angeles. We had only been to New York once, when we returned from India. We had been in Los

Angeles a number of times, but only when we just had to go to or through there.

One day while Phil was away, I was sitting in the living room looking around at everything. Suddenly, I had a strong urge to just pick up all of my precious furniture and throw it out of the window. "Oh!" I happily thought, "We must be going to go to Mexico!" I had always prayed that no matter where we went, I would be willing to leave that place and go wherever God said to go, for I always sincerely wanted to be in the center of God's will. There was no place that I'd rather go than to Mexico, so just thinking about going there brought great joy to my heart. Expectantly, I waited for Phil to come home and confirm my feelings; instead, he dealt me a blow when he announced, "We're moving to Los Angeles." Tears began to flow. I could scarcely believe my ears. Was God actually saying that we should move to one of the last places that either one of us ever wanted to live? But it was true. Phil said, "Let's start packing. We need to move while it is summer."

What had I liked about Mexico? The people, the language, the simplicity of life, sleeping on the mud floors, feeling the dirt between my toes. What could be better? God gave me the grace to follow my husband to L.A.

Chapter 29

Adventures in L. A. 1963–1968

—Helen—

During Phil's time in L.A., he had been with John Seymour and John's sister, Phyllis Gaunt. John and Phyllis were both working, but they had started holding services in their home, and we went to help them. John and Phyllis each had a separate bedroom, and there was one other bedroom for our family. Whenever company came, and there was plenty of it, we had a plan worked out. Phyllis strung wires in the living and dining rooms so that we could hang up sheets as dividers. With the sheets, we could actually make two divided rooms for the guests. In those days, John and Phil were doing a lot of teaching about the Tabernacle, so we would jokingly refer to our guest rooms as The Tabernacle.

We put our kids in a Christian school across town, so I soon became a freeway pro. I discovered, much to my joy, that not only was Los Angeles full of Mexicans, but people from every nation of the world were gathered there. I had thought that I wanted to go to Mexico; but God had a better plan for us. He not only wanted us to minister to Mexicans; but He wanted us to learn the ways and customs of the Asians. God had not forgotten the call He had given to Phil in Japan.

"For we walk by faith, not by sight"—2 Cor. 5:7

The time was getting close for us to answer that call, but first we needed much more training. God knew that living in Japan would be much different from living in Mexico, so He had sent us to Los Angeles to learn many things.

One special thing God taught me was how to spend money. It was very hard for me to spend as much as a dollar for our needs, for I tried to be very thrifty; but things were much more expensive in California. I had to spend more money in order to survive. When we went to Japan, things cost even more than in California. What we could buy for a dollar at home cost more like five or ten dollars. If I hadn't lived in Los Angeles, I would have had bigger problems living in Japan.

We began having frequent contact with Japanese and Chinese people, and we learned many helpful things from them. Some of the Chinese became lifelong friends and, amazingly, were some of our most faithful supporters when we were in Japan.

John, Phyllis, Phil, the children and I lived together for some time as the church was getting started. Later John and Phyllis moved to San Diego and started a work there while we pastored in Los Angeles. Our home became a little like Grand Central Station, and we greatly enjoyed it. Life was full of surprises. We never knew who might unexpectedly arrive at our door day or night, and we would receive them with open arms.

Noticing that much good food was being thrown away at a grocery store, we decided to ask if we could pick it up and use it. I began my daily route each weekday by taking the children to school in the morning (traveling over several freeways) and then picking them and the groceries up every afternoon. Since there would sometimes be several boxes of fruit and vegetables, the process of sorting the good from the bad was time consuming, but the food was a very real help in feeding our family and all our guests. If I had extra food, I would take it to Teen Challenge or some other place. We kept it in our garage. One time I noticed that a rat had gotten into the food, so I mentioned it to Phil; he said he would get some rat killer. The next morning I went to get something from the boxes and discovered a dead rat in one of them. "Oh Phil, you already put out the rat killer, didn't you," I said. "No," Phil responded. "I just decided to stand by the food and curse the rats." God let us actually see the dead rat to confirm that He had answered Phil's prayer. We were never bothered by rats there again.

Phil Writes

One fall we felt we should have a four-day convention. The church had no air conditioning, and that September turned out to be unseasonably hot, so we prayed that God would move the hot air out. He sent a mild hurricane to the west coast that moved the hot air out, and we had a cool convention.

Helen Continues

Before going to Los Angeles I sometimes wondered how a pastor could settle down in one place and pastor for many years; now, after pastoring such a precious group of people, I began to wonder if I ever wanted to go anywhere else again. Knowing that God had called me to the mission field, I distinctly remember one service we had. Philip Abraham, the precious pastor from India, was with us and had just finished preaching. He gave an altar call for those who wanted to surrender to God, but I was the only one who went forward. I cried out to God, "I know that I have a call on my life to go to other countries. Please help me to be willing to go when the time comes." Once again God heard my cry.

Nobuko Kitajima

As I mentioned, we had many visitors. Some would come and go, and some would stay awhile and receive some training. One time when Robert Ewing from Waco, Texas was with us, someone brought a young lady from Japan to meet us. Her name was Nobuko Kitajima. Robert spent quite a bit of time talking to her about Jesus; then he asked her if she would like to pray and ask Jesus into her heart. She agreed to pray, so Robert led her in prayer. Afterwards she was changed! She had been born again.

Later she explained what had really happened, "When Robert asked me about praying, I only said, 'Yes' out of politeness. While we were praying, I was picturing Buddha in my mind." In spite of this, God had seen her hungry heart and saved her.

Even though Nobuko spoke very little English, she began faithfully attending church. One morning she appeared at our house saying, "Please pray for me, because my heart hurts." We earnestly began praying for her healing, and she began speaking in tongues! She had wanted to be filled with the Spirit but hadn't known how to ask. God had blessed her simple faith, because from the time she came and asked for prayer until the time she left, she had only been in our home for five minutes! Nobuko became the best soul-winner in the church. One day she even called me on the phone and asked me to tell a Mexican about Jesus, because she couldn't speak any Spanish herself. After Nobuko returned to Japan, she became a fruitful worker there, too.

After about four and a half delightful years in Los Angeles, the time for the fulfillment of Phil's dream was about to be realized. Twenty-two years earlier when Phil was coming home on the troop ship from Japan, God had given him the dream about delivering the Japanese people from their harmful idol worship. We almost felt like Abraham who had waited so long for Isaac to be born, because we had tried to go to Japan twice earlier, only to be turned back by the hand of the Lord. But now the time had come, and we could hardly wait to go.

In 1968 Phil and Bobby Martz made a preliminary trip to Japan to "spy out the land". On the way they stopped by Hawaii. While there, they attended a Japanese picnic. We could tell that Phil hadn't enjoyed the food very much when later he told us, "It was the worst food I have ever eaten." However, God had a surprise for him. As he continued his trip on Japan Airlines, the Lord spoke to him saying, "I am giving you a liking for Japanese food." Soon after, a hostess came through the plane and asked if he would like some Japanese food. Believing what God had just spoken to him a few minutes earlier, he answered, "Yes." He says, "Soon she brought me a tray of raw fish, raw squid and raw octopus. I ate it down 1, 2, 3, 4, 5 with no trouble; and I have had no trouble with Japanese food since then." This was a wonderful preparation for traveling in Japan.

While in Japan Phil was amazed to see a "For Rent" sign in English on a house; I think this acted as a further confirmation that it was God's time to move. He was able to arrange for a young man to be our interpreter before he left Japan.

During the time that Phil was away, I bought some workbooks and started trying to learn Japanese. Yoko Isomine, the wife of a Japanese couple in the church, started teaching the girls and me the two Japanese alphabets. I had an insatiable appetite for the language, and I really appreciated each person who tried to help me learn. It was a real help to at least know the alphabets when we arrived in Japan, for all the signs were written in Japanese.

Tearfully saying goodbye, Jon, Sarah and Rachel found it hard to leave their friends behind, but they boarded the plane with us for their new adventure. Three big barrels and several trunks filled with school books and belongings were being shipped ahead of us.

Bethesda Gospel Church

Chapter 30

Life in Japan

—Helen—

In Tokyo we were met by the young man who had agreed to be our interpreter. He soon became more like a family member. Masayoshi (John) Fukuda proved to be an excellent teacher, guide, son, brother and companion. We did our best to keep up with him as he quickly guided us by train through Tokyo and on to Hino, which was about an hour away. Hino was the place where Jack and Edna Locker* had started a church, but Kato San** was now the pastor.

Suddenly we had been cast into a different world with many new customs, and our family felt a little awkward as we ate our first meal together with the church after service. To begin with, some of us were still half asleep. Another problem was that we were all seated in a circle, so that everyone could see us as we tried eating with chopsticks. Rachel was surprised when she tried to take a bite of food while standing up and was told that you were never supposed to eat anything unless you were seated!

*Jack and Edna Locker were the Ewings' son-in-law and daughter.

**San stands for Mr., Mrs., and Miss in Japanese, and it is almost always added to every name, unless there is another honorary addition like Sensei for teacher or Chan for children. I was called by Helen San in Japan to differentiate me from Phil who became Stanley San.

As our time in Japan continued, we enjoyed picking up our bowls and slurping noodles into our mouths; this is one thing we had been taught not to do in America. Men were always served before women, and we learned that you were supposed to reach across the table for your food instead of asking to have it passed. Our motto became, "If you don't know what you should do, just do the opposite of what you would do in America!"

After a few days, we were on our way to the town where we would spend the next two years. Hamakita was about an hour away from Mt. Fuji and about twenty minutes from Tenryu where the Bostrom family lived and had a church. The Bostroms, a veteran missionary family with five children, were a great blessing in helping us get started. We worked out of the Tenryu church.

The Bostrom and Stanley Families
Sachiko San (The Bostrom's Interpreter and a school girl are on the left in the middle row).

Our house was Japanese style with tatami (straw mat) floors and removable sliding doors. There was one room upstairs for the girls and one tiny room that Fukuda San and Jon shared downstairs. Phil and I would put our futons down on the tatami floors each night in what were used as the living/sitting rooms in the daytime.

There was a big shed on the side of the house which we had asked to be torn down so that Jon could plant a garden; but soon after the men started tearing it down, we realized our mistake and stopped them. That shed became the best part of the whole house, for our children spent hours playing ping pong there with students who came to visit us. (Our children can still beat almost anyone at ping pong because of their time in Hamakita.)

Fishing with Different Kinds of Bait

Fishing for souls and fishing for fish are very much alike. Jesus said, "I will make you fishers of men." Fishing takes time and patience. We found that English was very good bait. Students were required to take six years of English in school, but since even most of the teachers had no contact with English speakers, teachers and students alike really wanted to practice English with a native speaker. Students of all ages would come peeking around the corner at the end of the block, or even come to the door to see how we lived, talked, looked and ate. Of course, we would invite them in if we saw them, even if they were around the corner.

Since Japanese can't tell the difference between the pronunciation of "L" and "R", it sometimes presented some challenges. One girl came to our house and said that she had come to "p_ay." I couldn't tell if she was saying to play or to pray. I thought, "Shall I talk to her about God, or just visit with her?" After feeling my way for a few minutes, I decided that she had just come to "play." The Japanese word for play can also mean visit.

There was a similar problem the first time that Fukuda San interpreted Phil's message. Phil was preaching about the terrible plagues of Egypt, and how God had turned the dust into lice. Fukuda San said that God had turned the dust into "rice"! I think the impact of the terrible judgment was lost as the Japanese pictured the dust turning into their favorite food that they ate three times a day!

You would think nothing would scare me after driving the freeways of Los Angeles, but I was petrified when we first started riding in the car in Japan. It was three weeks before we could get a driver's license ourselves; meanwhile I would just sit in the back seat praying with my eyes closed, while our interpreter drove. Open sewers were on each side of the narrow streets; and since there were no sidewalks, people would be walking on the edges of the roads. It was scary! Finally, Phil and I got our licenses; but before I ever got to drive, it was time for Phil and Fukuda San to leave on their first ministry trip. They boarded the train one night after service, and I was supposed to drive someone home. As I began driving in the dark, I was shaking. Suddenly, I found myself singing a song, "His eye is on the sparrow, and I know He watches me." It was like God's great big hand reached down and took out all fear, and I had no trouble driving after that.

> 神は愛なり

One of the first things Fukuda San did was to make a huge banner in Japanese to hang in our living room. It said, GOD IS LOVE. We were told that the Japanese had a hard time understanding the concept of love, so that was a very important message for all who came to our home to see.

This was a time when Japan was really wide open for the gospel, for we had no trouble even getting into the schools and sharing about Jesus in the English clubs. People would listen, but they were very slow to believe.

Phil and Fukuda San were traveling much of the time. At first, it seemed like the Japanese were reluctant to invite Phil to their churches, for they thought that they would have to put him up in a hotel and provide special food for him. When they heard that he would eat their food and sleep on the floor in their homes, the doors became wide open. Quite a number of people in the churches had not yet received the baptism in the Holy Spirit, including some of the pastors. What a pleasure it was for him to see many of them filled!

In those days, many people had no place in their homes to take a bath; so it was necessary to go to the public bath houses. Phil had the experience of bathing at a bath house long before I did, for it took me quite a while to get up the courage to try one, since they were far from private. The side for the men and the side for the women would only be separated by one flimsy straw mat wall in between. Either a man or a woman would sit at the front taking the money from both the men and the women, and that person had the ability to watch both sides! On one occasion a group of Youth With a Mission (YWAM) girls went to a bath house and noticed that the wall looked unstable; one of the girls put her hand on the wall to stabilize it. The wall came tumbling down, exposing those on both sides to each other!

Since Phil was away a lot of the time, I started having Saturday afternoon English classes for high school students. One of the Bostroms' interpreters helped me. Sachiko San was both a friend and helper. English class consisted of singing some Christian choruses, a lesson from the Bible, and then some questions. One afternoon I was teaching about The Prodigal Son. Having observed in America how muddy pigs can get as they eat the scrap food that is thrown out to them, I was enlarging on the ugliness of sin by comparing it to the dirty pigs. One of the students raised his hand and then uttered a shocking statement to me, "Pigs aren't dirty." It turned out that his family raised pigs and they kept them very clean. After hearing that statement, I made this mental note, "That boy will never get saved!" What a mistake I had made. That boy, Shigeharu Kishita, not only accepted Christ as his Savior; he later became our interpreter for many years, and then became a pastor. So much for my carnal imaginations! In fact, two fulltime gospel workers came out of those English classes.

"Why don't you start a cooking class?" piped up Fukuda San one day. "The ladies would be interested in learning Western cooking." This was the beginning of many interesting experiences that included both laughs and tears. I, not being an exceptional cook, really had to pray and work hard to come up with something good. To begin with, the stove in a Japanese home only consisted of a two or three-burner hot plate. There were no ovens, and even though after a while the Bostroms gave us an old Coleman camping oven which we enjoyed using, it wasn't something that I could use to teach cooking to the ladies, for they had no ovens. The Lord helped me to learn how to make corn bread, biscuits, cookies, gingerbread, and more on top of the stove. In the class I would put something on to cook. While it was cooking I would give a Bible study; then we would eat what was cooked. In this way, I was able to share the gospel with a number of ladies. I had a cooking class during most of the years that we lived in Japan. One embarrassing time was when I made chicken and dumplings. When I raised the lid of the pan to serve the ladies, all of the dumplings had disintegrated. I had put them in too much water!

After almost two years in Japan, the Lord led Phil to go on a fast for seven days. As he prayed, he felt we should return to the States. That was almost the last thing that either of us wanted to hear, but we soon found out that God had a reason.

"For we walk by faith, not by sight"—2 Cor. 5:7

Chapter 31

Is She Dying?

—Philip—

During those first two years in Japan, God was doing a wonderful work in my life. I had always put other Christians and unbelievers first and my family last. God told me to start putting my family first. I had been putting others before my family for sixteen years. Surely, my family was neglected and many times condemned; but I did begin working on trying to change. God is merciful and forgiving. It wasn't very easy, but slowly I did change. I also began to teach and preach to others that they should put their families first.

Another thing that God began dealing with me about during our years in Japan was sectarianism. Without realizing it, I had developed the idea that I and the group I had fellowship with were the only ones who had the right doctrine. God began to show me that there were many of God's children who were very precious, and they had a lot of truth, also. I didn't have it all. We began to fellowship with other parts of the body of Christ. Praise God, I was delivered from being sectarian!

—Helen—

Phil and Fukuda San had made a trip to Indonesia. It had seemed as though the people there were much more receptive to the gospel than the people in Japan had been, so Phil decided that we should move to Indonesia when we finished our trip to the States. The Bostroms let us store at their place the things we would need for living in Indonesia. We began getting rid of everything else before going home.

Upon our arrival in the States, we spent a short time in Los Angeles before heading on to Dallas where my parents lived. We had only been with Mother a day or two when she suddenly collapsed and began hemorrhaging blood from her mouth. I thought she was dying, so I began quoting Psalm 23 to her, including the part that says, "Though I walk through the valley of the shadow of death, I will fear no evil..." My reasoning was, "If I were dying, that's something that I would like for someone to quote to me." Mother told me later that God was saying something different to her. She was hearing, "I am the resurrection and the life."

We called an ambulance and Mother was taken to the hospital where she learned that she had a bleeding stomach ulcer. True to God's Word, she recuperated; but the Lord had us in the States for two years. During that time, we moved Mother to Waco, Texas, so that the girls could attend a Christian school there while I helped nurse Mother back to health.

I figured that I should learn some Indonesian if we were going to move there. In my spare time, I bought a language study book and began trying to learn it; meanwhile, Phil was ministering in various places in and out of the States. Our son Jonathan completed his high school correspondence course and moved to Los Angeles.

As time went by, Phil began to realize that God wanted us to return to Japan instead of going to Indonesia. We wanted to be sure that Mother had a good place to live, so my sister and I bought a house near the church that was reasonable, but it needed some remodeling. Even though we hired someone to do the work, Phil and I both pitched in to try to help so that we could save some money. Neither Phil nor I knew anything about painting or carpentry, but, unbeknown to us, it was an excellent learning time that would prove to be very profitable in the near future.

As Phil describes his experience: "At that time God, was teaching me the true meaning of I Thessalonians 5:18. I was up on the roof of the house hammering nails, when suddenly I hit my thumb with the hammer. God said, 'In everything give thanks.' I did, and that was the beginning of my giving thanks in every circumstance. Oh, that has been such a help to me in my praise and worship of the Lord!"

Chapter 32

Back to Japan

—Helen—

As we were traveling on a ministry trip shortly before returning to Japan, the Lord made a scripture passage real to me, and I remember testifying about it. "*By faith Abraham obeyed when he was called to go out to the place which he would receive as an inheritance; And he went out, not knowing where he was going...*" (Heb. 11:8). I really felt like the parts that said "...not knowing where he was going..." and "...after receive (it) for an inheritance." expressed our feeling perfectly. The promise was wonderful, but where was that place? We needed to know where God wanted us in Japan. We felt it was now time to launch out and start a church in a new place.

About three weeks before moving to Japan we were once again in our car on the way to some meetings. Phil began asking God to show him where we were to settle. God impressed Hiroshima Prefecture* on him. His first reaction was, "I wonder if they like Americans there?" He didn't say anything to me about his thoughts, but he asked God to confirm it to him.

*A prefecture in Japan is like a state in the U.S. or a province in Canada.

—Philip—

About thirty minutes later, Helen suddenly turned on the car radio—something she never did! The first thing we heard was a news commentator talking about Hiroshima Prefecture. In his comments, he mentioned the name of a Japanese lady who had visited the church in Los Angeles during our time of pastoring there. We knew she was from Hiroshima. I then told Helen what God had been speaking to me. This was a confirmation to both of us that Hiroshima Prefecture was where God wanted us to be. Helen also wondered if we would be welcome in that area, but there was nothing to worry about. We were treated like kings and queens all the time we lived in Japan, even in the Hiroshima area.

—Helen—

Before leaving the U.S., there were two big decisions facing us. One was the fact that only about a year remained before our girls would graduate from high school. Should they go with us to Japan, or stay in the States to study? The decision was made that they would stay in the States for some months, and then join us in Japan later. But as Phil and I were driving to California, Phil began feeling impressed that they should fly out to California to meet us; then we could all go together to Japan. We made the call and told them to come, but after we arrived in California I was still very troubled. "Had we made the right decision?" From the depths of my heart, I cried out with tears to God for an answer. As I opened my Bible to read, my eyes fell on Zechariah 10:7: "*Those of Ephraim shall be like a mighty man, And their heart shall rejoice as if with wine. Yes, their children shall see it and be glad; Their heart shall rejoice in the Lord.*" The next morning when I read the chapter again, I noticed verse 9 in the same chapter: "*I will sow them among the peoples, And they shall remember Me in far countries; They shall live, together with their children, And they shall return.*" These scriptures brought great peace to my heart. At the same time God gave me the scripture about our girls, He said, "There is also a confirmation of the city in which you are to live after you arrive in Japan." Just a few weeks later we were really going to need the confirmation that we were in God's will.

There was one more heartbreaking problem that faced us. Jonathan had gotten snared by drugs in Los Angeles and had begun saying he no longer believed in God. This had been weighing on our hearts for quite some time, and we had prayed fervently for him. A few months earlier when we had been in a conference in California, the people had been singing the scripture song from Isaiah 55:12: "*For you shall go out with joy, And be led forth with peace: the mountains and the hills Shall break forth into singing before you, And all the trees of the field shall clap their hands.*" Shortly before that conference I had read Merlin R. Carothers's book *Prison to Praise*. It had made an impact on me, and now I decided to put what I had read into practice. Even though Phil would occasionally dance before the Lord in those days, I had been too bashful to do so. However, in that service I looked around and saw many people dancing and rejoicing. I thought, "I am just going to dance and praise God for the circumstances surrounding Jonathan. Even though things look awful, I'm going to wholeheartedly dance and give thanks to God for them." Phil had also been praising God for the victory. We found that God really works through praise!

One day soon after we arrived in Los Angeles on our way to Japan, Jon thought he was dying. As I held his head in my lap, he repented and returned to God. He has never departed from God again. In fact, he answered his call to the ministry and has ministered in various ways since that time. He didn't go back to Japan with us. Instead we put him on a plane to Waco, and he stayed with my mother until he married sometime later.

Chapter 33

Is This the Right Place?

—Philip—

Returning to the area where we had lived previously in Japan, we got our things out of storage. In the process, an old car was given to us by some missionaries from the Nagoya area. Another missionary, Bill Mollenkamp, was able to borrow a small truck and help move our things. As we got to Hiroshima Prefecture, we had to decide which city to live in. We had confidence the Lord would show us. First we stopped to inquire at a city called Fukuyama. From Fukuyama we turned inland and began climbing up a narrow mountain road until we reached a place called Fuchu; here we stopped again to inquire. Finally, we reached a place called Miyoshi. It seemed that the Lord was giving us the witness that this was where we should live, so we started to look for a place to rent. A real estate agent took us to the only three available houses. One was like a shed; the second one was next to the Buddhist Temple; and the third one was on a hillside just outside of town. It had been used for a company dormitory. The last one is the one I felt we should take, but when I told Helen she said, "I don't feel good about that house." I answered, "I don't think we will be there long." Then she said, "OK" and that she felt all right about it.

—Helen: Why Such a Short Time?—

The house we moved into was just outside the city. It sat on the side of a mountain, only about five or ten yards from the highway—just enough good space there to park our car. On the other side of the highway was a river. The house directly across the street from us was built so that when you took a step out of the front door, you stepped onto the highway pavement. The story underneath was built hanging over the river.

It was dark in our house. A little stream flowed down the left side of it, and the mountainside behind was covered with trees. When we were upstairs

we could see the snake that lived in the tree right outside the back window. We killed a number of large centipedes during the three weeks we lived there.

As I looked at the river across from us one day, I distinctly remember

thinking, "I usually put off taking pictures, but I think I'm going to get my camera right now and take a picture of that river. It looks so beautiful, serenely flowing by." I'm glad I put some feet to my thoughts, for soon that scene would forever change.

We anxiously awaited the arrival of our possessions from America. We had received notice that the things had arrived in

Japan, but the Bill of Lading hadn't yet come; also, no money was arriving. During the waiting period, we decided to drive to the marine base in Iwakuni to meet some missionaries we had heard about. At the end of the three-hour trip, we were warmly met by Don and Grace Bowman and were deeply touched as we listened to their story.

Some years earlier, Don and Grace had ordered a ship to be built so they could sail to some of the over 426 inhabited islands of Japan to share the gospel. On the ship's maiden voyage it had sprung a leak and had sunk; all four of the Bowman children had drowned, along with an American sailor and a Japanese man. Only Don and Grace had survived, and their survival had been miraculous. Since that horrific loss, God had graciously given them three more children, and they just happened to be celebrating the birthday of their youngest girl that day when we were with them.

The Bowmans helped us get some chests of drawers and a rattan couch and chairs from the base. Even though the things had been sitting out in the rain, we were still able to get years of wear out of them.

Now that we had some furniture, we were praying more and more for money and for the Bill of Lading to arrive so that we could pick up the things we had shipped. I needed to get material to cover the furniture and make curtains. We needed to fix up the house.

I hadn't read anything but the Bible for a number of years, but for some reason I read three books in three weeks' time. Each book was about missionaries who had suffered great loss. One of the books was *Through Gates of Splendor*, about how five missionaries had given their lives in Ecuador. Another one was *How I Know God Answers Prayer*, by Rosalind Goforth. The Goforths were missionaries who had lost five of their eleven children either at birth or when they were still young. It seemed as though God was preparing me for something. I would sometimes look out the window and feel that some trial was coming, but I didn't know what it would be.

During our third week in the house, we decided it was time to start having service, so we began making an announcement to get printed. We planned to begin services the following Sunday. At the end of the week, the Lord reminded me of the scripture He had given me in Zechariah 10, about our children living with us in other lands. He had said that there was also a confirmation of where we were to live in Japan in that same chapter, so I decided I had better study it and see what the Lord was saying. As I began looking up some of the meanings of the words, I saw that it was a perfect picture of Miyoshi.

Finally, the Bill of Lading arrived—it had mistakenly been sent to my mother's house in Texas instead of to Japan. We all rejoiced, and it was decided that Phil and Kishita San would leave on Tuesday afternoon to pick up our things in Kobe.

We had been spending time in fasting and prayer in preparation for the opening of the church services. The girls were going to have their first English class on Tuesday morning. On Monday God gave me a wonderful promise in Acts 7:34. *"I have seen, I have seen the affliction of my people which is in Egypt, and I have heard their groaning, and am come down to deliver them. And now come, I will send you into Egypt."*

"How was this going to happen? What was God talking about?" I wondered.

That same day something else of significance happened. The girls and I discovered a path over the mountain that led from our house to the highway below. This was something that we would need to know the next day.

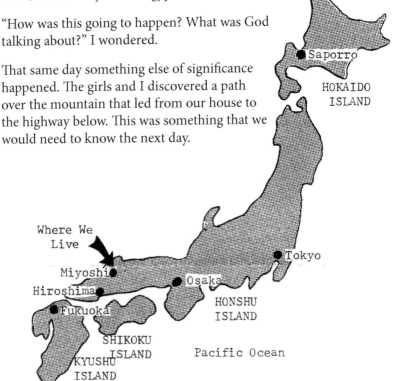

Chapter 34

The Flood

—Helen—

At 5:00 a.m. Tuesday we heard Kishita San leap out of his futon shouting, "Flood!" It had been raining hard since Sunday, but a flood had not entered our minds. Now someone in a car was driving down the highway to warn the people over a loudspeaker. The English class and the trip to pick up our possessions were canceled.

As the day wore on, we saw that some of the houses just down the highway from us toward town had water seeping in, for their homes were also built up to the highway. Even though our house was on a mountainside, I never realized that we might be in danger, but Phil was sensing the urgency of the situation. At one point he even considered moving to higher ground.

Our neighbors across the street moved some of their things into our house, then the husband went back to stand watch over the river. His wife and daughter ate breakfast with us and then went home about eleven a.m. In the afternoon, the city opened the flood gates to keep the dam from breaking, and a small landslide covered the highway about a block away. (There were three rivers in the city.) Our neighbor's wife and daughter came over again in the afternoon and later decided to spend the night with us, while the husband continued to stand watch over the river.

Trying to find some way to minister to our neighbors, I put on a tape that I thought had some Japanese music on it. As I was skipping through the tape, I would stop ever so often to try to find that music, but I never found it. Instead, it was a recording of some convention in Texas. Each time I would stop the tape to check to see if I had reached the Japanese music, I would hear something interesting. In one place, the congregation was singing, "God Leads His Dear

Children Along." The chorus says, "Some through the water, some through the flood."  Next, we heard one of our friends singing something about "living on a mountain," and lastly, Phil came on the tape preaching from Psalm 23. Since there was a flood, we were living on the side of a mountain, and we certainly needed the care of a shepherd, I felt that God had been sending me a message via the tape.

About 10:00 p.m. the transformer for our area broke and we were in darkness except for candlelight; thirty minutes later we began moving our neighbors' furniture into our house, for the river was looking more ominous.

The neighbors' little girl was afraid, so I got out my accordion and began to sing. Suddenly, we heard a great cracking noise and the candles went out. We were in darkness. We thought the dam must have broken. Phil yelled to us to run upstairs. When Phil, Rachel, Kishita San and I arrived upstairs, Sarah was missing. I can still hear Phil's sad, mournful voice as he yelled, "Sa-a-rah! Sa-a-rah!" How we rejoiced when she appeared!

A landslide had come down the path of the little stream that ran by the side of the house.

The rocks covered the highway toward town, and about half of our car as well. Our front entrance was gone. That meant our shoes were missing, too, for it was the custom for everyone to take off their shoes before entering the house. Remembering the little path over the side of the mountain that we had just discovered the day before, we climbed out a downstairs window. Though barefooted, we were able to relocate the path and climb down to the highway below. Some neighbors about a block further down the highway heard the noise and came to lead us to their house, which was also built over the river. Other neighbors had gathered there as well.

For two days and two nights we wondered if we would live or die. I would look at the raging water and think of the chorus I had heard on the tape, "Some through the water; some through the flood." "Does that mean we are actually going to have to go through those waters?" I wondered. I remembered what I had read in Zechariah 10 when God had confirmed to me that we were in the right location. Verse 11 says, "And he shall pass through the sea with affliction, and shall smite the waves in the sea . . . " Well, I am glad to report that we were safe and didn't have to actually go through the water.

After two days with our neighbors, we were able to go back to our house and survey the situation. Before arriving there, we didn't know whether any of our possessions had survived the landslide or not. As I was walking along the highway toward the house I found myself singing, "If ever I loved Thee, my Jesus, 'tis now." Many times God's presence can be felt more in times of trial. I knew that God had carefully prepared me ahead of time by the books I had read and the songs and testimonies I had heard on the tape. I realized, too, that God had allowed this trial to get us quickly introduced to the people of that area.

As soon as the typhoon had passed, the son of the area chief came and invited us to stay on their property in a place that had just been built, but never lived in. Up over their garage they had built a large room that could be divided into two rooms by inserting sliding doors. The doors could be put in to make two rooms, or taken out when one large room was needed. Thankfully, there was a toilet, too.

The communities had another very nice custom. When some new person moved into the neighborhood, the newcomer would go to each house in the area to introduce himself, or herself; at that time the newcomer would give a small gift like a bar of soap or a hand towel to each of his new neighbors.

(Neighborhoods in Japan are presided over by an elected area chief who serves for a certain period of time, so he coordinates the various activities of the neighborhood. Neighbors are expected to work together to help families who are having a wedding, funeral, sickness, etc. Ever so often, the open sewers that ran in front of the houses would need to be cleaned. The neighbors would all work together to clean their sewers; this usually took place on Sunday morning. In the first place we lived, the different utility bills would be passed from house to house, so neighbors would have to have contact with each other. After all the money to pay the bills would be collected, the area chief would deliver it to the proper utility company. It was a nice system to keep neighbors connected.)

—Philip—

There were three rivers in Miyoshi. In the older part of the city, the area closest to us, the water came over the bank and flooded the houses, but in the main part of the city, the riverbank broke and the water reached up to the first floor ceilings. The whole city had to be renewed. The thick rice straw mats covering most of the floors in the houses all had to be thrown away.

A new chapter was opening in our lives. Our area chief invited us to stay with him, and he lived farther out into the country. We were given two upstairs rooms to rent that had never been lived in. Helen and I and our two daughters lived in the larger room, and the smaller one was for our interpreter. We used a tiny room downstairs for our kitchen. Since there was no running water, or even a sink in the downstairs room, we washed dishes at an outdoor faucet and cooked on a gas hot plate. When we moved in, we washed many of our things in a creek that ran in front of the house.

—Helen—

Our refrigerator, waffle iron, cassette tapes, shoes and everything from our former house were all packed with mud, for as much as two feet of mud covered some places. Amazingly most of the things still worked after much washing!

Just as we were going to enter the new place, Don Bowman (the missionary we had met only a few days earlier) arrived and offered to take us to their home in Iwakuni. He had been searching for us on foot for an hour and a half. The girls and I went with him, but Phil and Kishita San stayed behind to get what they could out of the house.

When Phil and Kishita finally arrived back, we heard more of how God had miraculously protected us. All the trees on the mountain behind us had been swept down by the landslide. In the narrow kitchen where Sarah and Rachel had been fixing tea, a big tree about a foot in diameter had come all the way through the kitchen. The girls don't know how they got out of the kitchen before being hit by the tree. In the living room where Phil had been, and where I had been playing the accordion for our neighbors, there was a rock the size of two basketballs put together; but no one had been hit by a rock or tree, except for one tiny rock that hit my leg.

In the living room, four large windows all in a row, were completely knocked out, but God allowed five trees to fall across the place where the windows had been. They had formed a natural barrier from the other rocks and trees that had come down the mountain. One rock that had been stopped by that barrier was too big for three men to move.

Phil and Rachel had bad cuts on their feet, but God helped their feet not to get too infected until the storm was over and they were able to soak their feet. Twelve people had lost their lives, and some of the houses near us had been swept away.

"For we walk by faith, not by sight"—2 Cor. 5:7

Chapter 35

Birth of Miyoshi Bible Church

—Helen—

The ladies at the marine base in Iwakuni invited me to share my testimony. After I finished speaking, they gave us a three-burner stove with a small oven, some shoes for Phil, since he had lost all of his in the landslide, and some other household articles. We felt very blessed!

After getting settled into our new location, we decided to have three days of special meetings in the two rooms upstairs where we stayed. By just taking out the sliding doors that divided the two rooms, we were able to accommodate the twenty-five or so people who came out that first service. This was the beginning of the church in Miyoshi. We continued having services there until we finally found a place to rent downtown over four months later.

The new place had been a maternity clinic. It consisted of living quarters for the doctor and his family, two rooms and a kitchen for the nurses, and the rooms for the hospital. It was right downtown. The place had been underwater up to the ceiling of the first floor, so Phil was able to arrange for cheaper rent for a period of time, if we would fix up the place. Now we understood why we had gotten some painting and carpentry experience just a short time earlier while helping remodel Mother's house!

In the beginning days, we only rented the doctor's and the nurses' sections of the building. The church meetings were held in a tatami* room in the nurses' quarters, and we all sat on the floor. Since it was somewhat the custom for the people to look down instead of looking at the speaker, we would often never know whether the people were asleep or awake. People came to the services, but they were slow to believe. In fact, Phil has said that sometimes in Japan he felt like he was holding up a dead man and speaking, "Live! Live!"

After a while, we were able to lease the whole building. When it came time to baptize the new believers, we discovered that the operating room was the perfect place—it had a tile floor with a drain in it. Phil had something made that resembled a metal coffin, so it looked like we were really burying the "old man of sin" when we baptized someone. It was always a time of rejoicing.

First baptisimal service took place at the river

*Tatami is the word used for the thick rice straw mats that cover the floor of a room. Each mat is about two inches thick, and the length and width of each one is just about the size of a futon that you lay on the floor on which to sleep. A realtor describes a room by the number of mats it contains.

—Philip—

After the three days of meetings, it was mostly the young people who kept coming to church; but the Lord impressed me to pray for young families. We asked God for couples who didn't yet have children, or for those who were just beginning a family. Also we prayed that God would give us people who would not move away. God began to answer our prayers by giving us young families. In smaller cities, it was very common for young people to soon move to the big cities when they finished high school or college. Also, the work system called for the workers to move every two years, if they wanted a promotion. One man in the church worked for the Electric Company. We agreed in prayer with him that he wouldn't have to move, and he was able to stay in Miyoshi for eight years. Another person worked for a large medical company. After a few years everyone in his group had to move to Osaka, but he didn't have to move until a number of years later.

A young man named Tsuji San got a job at a company that made all the doors for Japanese houses. Almost every home has a special place for the Buddhist altar where people worship their dead ancestors, with ornate doors that can be closed in front of the altar. When the young man applied for the job, he said that he would make all the doors except the ones for the altar. God gave him favor with his boss, and his request was granted. That young man is now pastoring a flourishing church in Hiroshima City.

When we first went to Miyoshi, we had an old car that would hardly run. In fact, one time with the girls' help we had to push our car out of the way when it stopped running right at the toll gate of the main freeway to Osaka. This helped force our faith, and soon we were able to buy an eight-seated Toyota van.

At the very beginning of our time in Miyoshi, we didn't have any money—so we prayed. God supplied our needs through unbelievers without our telling anyone about our need. Oh, how wonderful it is to trust the Lord!

—Helen—

So many things happened during our years in Miyoshi. Sarah and Rachel were with us at first, and they were a great help in reaching the young people, but after a year they returned to the States, and entered Portland Bible College in Portland, Oregon.

We started English classes and a ladies' cooking class again and used both events as outreaches. Some of the other outreaches included ladies' luncheons, men's dinners,

films, concerts, wiener roasts, tent meetings and distributing Gideon bi-lingual New Testaments to the schools. We covered all of Miyoshi with tracks.

Among some of the first new believers was a young lady named Junko who later became Kishita's wife; they later became pastors.

The Kishitas

"For we walk by faith, not by sight"—2 Cor. 5:7

Junko Tamuro Suzuki
Artist of sketches of pages 20-21

The Lord was good to send us another interpreter, also. Junko Tamuro Suzuki lived with us for many years. Junko received the Baptism of the Holy Spirit; then she told her sister about her experience and gave her the book *Nine O'clock in the Morning* to read. Her sister told God that she wanted the Baptism of the Holy Spirit for her birthday. We were excited to hear that God wonderfully answered her request.

We even found that God was mindful of our family. It isn't easy to be separated from your children by an ocean. In those days, overseas phone calls were expensive, and email and Skype were unknown. Videos were just beginning to be popular shortly before we returned to America. It usually took about a week to receive mail from our family, sometimes even two weeks. (Of course, we had it a lot better than the missionaries of long ago, when they sometimes waited months or even years without hearing anything!)

We were very thankful God made it possible for us to be home for Jonathan's wedding, but He had a surprise for us when our son called and said that

Reuben with other church babies

he and his wife Betty were going to come to Japan shortly before their first baby was to be born. Thus, it turned out that we had the privilege of having our first grandson delivered by a midwife in our home in Japan, so we were able to watch baby Reuben grow for the first nine months of his life.

Amber with Yoshiya Kishita

Shortly after Jon and Betty returned to the States, our younger daughter Rachel and her husband John came and spent nine months with us. Their first child, Amber, was about nine months old when they arrived in Japan. This meant that we had enjoyed the privilege of being with one of our grandchildren from the time of birth to the time of eighteen months. Only God could arrange something so perfectly! Both babies provided many opportunities to share the gospel.

After some years, our landlord sold the clinic and we needed to move. It was interesting that we had started the church in a former

Church at the former restrauant

maternity clinic—the "birthing place". When we first arrived in Miyoshi, we didn't know any other Christians, so our beginning ministry was teaching the very simple truths of salvation to the people who came. The next place we moved happened to be a former restaurant. The new believers now

Front and side view of the present church

"For we walk by faith, not by sight"—2 Cor. 5:7 • 143

Present Pastor Suemune, Former Pastor Kishita and the Stanleys, Founding Pastors

needed more spiritual "meat" to grow. It seemed very fitting that we had moved to the "feeding place." After the restaurant, the church was able to move to a permanent location and build their own church building. This last move took place after we returned to the States.

Chapter 36

As Birds Flying: 1983

—Helen—

A few years before we moved home, Phil became very sick. He couldn't preach, and he could hardly eat. As we were praying earnestly about what to do, we took a step of faith and went to the annual Pentecostal Pastors' Conference in Tokyo. Phil could barely make it. Pastor Dick Iverson from Portland, Oregon happened to be the speaker that evening. As Phil went up for prayer after the service, Pastor Iverson told Phil that he needed to rest. He even said, "Come to Portland for a year." This seemed to be a confirmation of a scripture that the Lord had given me when we had been praying about what to do. *"Like birds flying about, So will the Lord of hosts defend Jerusalem. Defending, He will also deliver it; Passing over, He will preserve it."* (Isa. 31:5). The very next morning I put Phil on the plane bound for Portland, and the girls met him at the airport. They had contacted a doctor named David Blessing. The doctor discovered that Phil's problem was his heart; he put him on medication and told him to start walking daily. True to his name, David Blessing was a blessing. He continues to be a blessing as our family doctor until this day. *"Like birds flying,"* Phil had boarded an airplane and gone home. Phil was delivered, and he has been preserved even until now. God has such interesting ways to reveal His will to us.

After the conference, I went back to Miyoshi to pack and tie up loose ends before flying to Portland a month later. How good it was to be able to spend a whole year with our two daughters and their families! Being with them was not only a pleasure—it was like a strengthening, healing medicine. Families are important. As soon as Phil arrived home and was able to lay down the burden of caring for the church, his health began to improve. He only preached two or three times that year; but after that he was able to take up the burden again.

Another scripture the Lord had given to Phil and me just before he went home was Ps 68:1: "*Let God arise, Let His enemies be scattered: Let those also who hate Him flee before Him.*" The first Sunday after I arrived in Portland, the morning message was about that scripture. We went to a home meeting that night, and the first song they sang there was that same scripture verse. God knows how to confirm His will to us.

Just after we arrived back in the States, we unexpectedly received a large amount of money; this helped take care of our needs that year. God, our Heavenly Father, had prepared everything for us ahead of time. Besides that, the church let us stay all that year in one of the apartments they owned.

When I would drive around the area where we were staying, I would notice quite a number of foreigners, but I couldn't identify from which country they had come. One Sunday after church I thought, "I'm going to drive around and see if I can find where they all live, but first I want to take a short nap." I lay down on the bed, but I began to itch, so I thought, "I'm going to get up and pray some before I go." I got on my knees to pray, but immediately I started itching again. I decided I had better just get up and go!

I drove around for some time without seeing a single one of those special foreigners, so it seemed time to go home. As I was driving along a busy street on the way back, a sign on a church window caught my attention. I parked my car and went back to read the sign. It said that a Japanese service was being held right then! Immediately I went into the service, knowing that God had led me there. If I had first taken a nap, I would never have found that service. As it was, I continued going to that Japanese service each Sunday while we were in Portland. It was God's way of saying to me, "You're not through in Japan yet!"

Some years later I learned that the people whom I had seen were Laotians, and I had driven very close to where there was a whole settlement of them. In fact, there is a Laotian service now at City Bible Church where we attend.

Chapter 37

God Answers a Big Request

—Helen—

After the year in the States was up, we returned to Miyoshi. Not long after that, Phil felt it was time to install a Japanese pastor, so our former interpreter, Shigeharu Kishita, became the pastor. We moved into a house away from the church and began a traveling ministry again.

We would go back to the States from time to time, but there would always be a question about our aging parents when it came time to return to Japan. Both of our mothers lived alone—how much longer could we leave them? We prayed that God would help all of our parents have a sound mind when they died and that we would be with them. That was a big request seeing that we lived across the ocean. After about two more years in Miyoshi, the day arrived when Phil said, "I feel like it is time to move back to the States and use that as a base to continue traveling to the nations."

Once again we began packing our things in big barrels so that we could ship home the things we really wanted to keep. Everything else was either sold or given away. We weren't sure where we would actually move, but as time went by it seemed that Portland, Oregon, was the place we were to be. A few years earlier we had moved Phil's mother there from California so that Sarah and Rachel, who both lived in Portland, could watch over them. Bible Temple (now City Bible Church) was the church we thought we should attend. We had worked out of Grace Bible Church in Honolulu, Hawaii, for a number of years, and they had been very supportive.

We very much appreciate all that Pastor Sam Webb and the church in Honolulu did for us.

Sam and Nancy Webb with the Grace Bible Church staff.

Soon after arriving in Portland, our barrels arrived from Japan. I well remember the telephone call I received from my sister that morning when I was unpacking the barrels. Her first words were, "Doc just died." Doc, Marian's husband, had not been sick at all, so it was very unexpected. How thankful I was that we were home in the States. I got on a plane and flew to my sister's home in Texas as soon as possible. What a blessing it was to be able to spend a week or two with her.

Thomas Harvey Stanley

Phil's father had died at the age of sixty-two while we were still living in Los Angeles. Phil and I were quite tired from the daily demands of pastoring, so we had really been looking forward to a short vacation on a farm that was owned by some Chinese friends of ours. The children were loaded in the car, along with all of our bags, and we had started on our way. Suddenly, Phil began feeling that he should just stop by to see his father, who was in the hospital, even though we would only be gone a few days. When Phil arrived at his father's room, he discovered that a piece of an X-ray machine had fallen on

148 • Adventures in Faith

his father's face, and his father's condition had worsened. Needless to say, we cancelled our vacation and stayed with his father, who died a short time later.

Now years later in Portland, Phil's mother had become quite wobbly. We thought it would be good for her to live with us, so we moved her into our home. After a period of time, we heard that my mother had fallen and broken her hip in Texas and was recovering in a nursing home. We made a trip to Texas to help my sister have an estate sale and sell Mother's house. After taking care of things there, we brought my mother back to Portland so she, too, could live with us. It was quite an experience having two mothers with two different personalities both living together with us, and it worked out for a while. However, before long Phil's mother decided to move back into an apartment of her own. She stayed there until she just got unable to take care of herself any longer.

My mother fell again and broke her other hip. Now I was really reluctant to let her do things by herself, but her care became more than I could easily do by myself. We began thinking it was time for her to go into a foster home. The Lord provided a wonderful Christian home where she was in the loving care of a Romanian pastor's wife. This allowed us to spend more relaxed times together with her. Instead of being responsible for all of her daily care, we could visit her, bring her to our house, take her to church or family gatherings, or even play games together.

A few months before Thanksgiving, 1993, I felt the Lord tell me to be extra nice to my mother, for He was going to take her home soon.

Frances Mary Briley

I had always tried to be nice, for I loved her very much. She was a very sweet mother who never got mad at me. In fact, one of her favorite verses was Ps. 119:165: "*Great peace have they which love thy law: and nothing shall offend them.*" (KVJ). Mother spent Thanksgiving together with all our family. We were getting ready to pick Mother up for the Sunday morning service when we received a call from the foster home that she was unconscious. She revived shortly after we arrived. She didn't want to go to the doctor on Sunday, so I played Scrabble with her until later in the day, when she decided to go to the hospital. I was with her when she went to be with the Lord in the wee hours of Monday morning. She was 91.

My father had died four years earlier. He and his wife lived in Dallas, Texas. Since our son and his family lived in Louisiana and my sister lived in Austin, we would try from time to time to drive to their respective places to spend some time with each of them when we were down south. At this particular time, we had visited our son and his family and were on our way to see my sister. Our last planned stop would be to see Dad; however, God spoke to Phil and said that we should go straight to Dallas. Right then and there we changed our direction. We had supper with Dad and Pearl, his wife, and later retired to bed. During the night, Dad woke us up and asked us to call his good friends next door and ask them to call an ambulance to come get him. We thought this was very strange. "Why should we wake up his neighbors when we are right here? We could easily call the ambulance ourselves," we thought. We called the neighbors and they came over. Later we understood that was Dad's way of telling them goodbye.

I went with Dad to the hospital and spent the day with him. Since Dad had been sick many times with heart trouble, I had no idea that this time was different. He always really worried if Marian and I were out late at night, so I felt it would be good to go home before it got too late. As I kissed him goodnight, he gave me the sweetest look. The next morning as I was preparing to return to see him, we received a call from the hospital. Dad had gone home to Jesus.

Pearl and JJ Briley

The day of the funeral I woke up with a scripture song ringing in my heart. *"This is the day which the LORD has made; we will rejoice and be glad in it"* (Ps. 118:24). Our daughters had flown down from

Portland for the funeral, and they brought our mail with them. After the service was over, I started looking at the mail. Imagine my amazement when I opened an envelope and pulled out a greeting card that looked like this.

> *This Is The Day*
> *That The Lord*
> *Has Made*
> *Let Us Rejoice*
> *And Be*
> *Glad In It!*

That card was from someone I hadn't heard from in at least a year, and they knew nothing about what had transpired. What a great comfort and confirmation it was to me to be reassured that Dad was with Jesus.

Dad's wife Pearl had died just a few days before my mother had died. Even though I wasn't with her on that day, I had just had a good visit with her in Texas a few days earlier, for which I was very thankful. I was not able to attend her funeral because of Mother's passing.

As Phil's mother became feebler, we were able to find a good Christian foster home for her, too. She fell two different times and broke a hip each time. However, even though her mind was still good, she would forget that she had broken her hip. She would get right up and start walking again when her hip healed. The way that God opened up the way for us to be with her when God called her home was amazing!

"For we walk by faith, not by sight"—2 Cor. 5:7

Chapter 38

There's That Old Mosquito!

—Helen—

For some years I hadn't traveled much with Phil, due to caring for our mothers over a long period of time, but once again I had started accompanying him. This particular time we went to India to help Dale and Mary Sexauer for two weeks in one of their campaigns in the Punjab. It was a real blessing to see how God moved in healing and delivering people, and the leaders of the village were quite open by even inviting us into one of their homes for a meal. As we would walk through the village during the day, there would be shouts of "Hallelujah" as someone would recount how they had been healed. Phil likes to tell about the tiny church that only held about fifty people before the meetings, but the first Sunday after the meetings, there were about 2,000 hungry hearts that came to hear the Word. The service was held outside the church while the people gathered around.

We had flown into New Delhi and planned to return home from there, but first we were scheduled to go down south for two meetings. The telephone service was not good in parts of India, so we hadn't been in contact with our family for the two weeks we had been in the Punjab. It seemed to be a good idea to just call home to see how things were while we were in New Delhi, for the telephone connection was good there; but when we started to call, we realized

that it was still the wee hours of the morning at home. Phil was tired and had gone to bed without eating that evening, so after a while I decided to do the same. As I turned out the light and crawled into bed, I heard a mosquito buzzing around. "I'll never be able to sleep until I get rid of that mosquito," I thought. I got out of bed and turned on the light. Then I heard our hostess calling, "Would you like something to eat?" Since the truth was that I really did want something to eat, I got up, had something to eat, visited a little longer, and started back to bed.

It was then that I looked at my watch and noticed that now it wasn't too early to call home. Our daughter, Sarah, answered the phone and I asked, "How is everything at home?" fully expecting her usual

"Everything is just fine!" Instead she said, "Grandmother is dying." Well, we were right where we needed to be. The next morning we cancelled our trip to the south, changed our tickets, and flew home to Portland that same day. We were able to be with Mother until she went to be with Jesus two weeks later. That was the first time we were able to really give thanks for a mosquito! God's messages sometime come through strange messengers!

"For we walk by faith, not by sight"—2 Cor. 5:7

Chapter 39

The Deep, Dark Trial

—Helen—

Phil had been traveling to many places while I had been taking care of our mothers. He had made trips back to Japan, Mexico and India, and he had gone to new places like Iceland, Burma and Europe. Now I was free to travel with him once again.

Actually, even though I was very happy on the one hand, I had been going through a deep, dark trial on the other hand. The trial concerned my ministry. Before ever meeting Phil, I had felt a call to the mission field, and I had been active in some form of ministry most of the time throughout the years. However, there had been a great change after we turned the church in Miyoshi over to a Japanese pastor. It was as though I was out of a job, for we wanted to let the new pastor and his wife begin to take responsibility. We had started traveling in Japan again. Phil was speaking at the different churches, counseling, and being very fulfilled in his ministry. I, however, was sitting, listening, and sitting again. I would offer to help serve, do dishes, or do whatever else I could do to help our hostess wherever we would go; but wanting to be kind to me, our hostess would graciously refuse my help, since I was the guest. I understood her desire to let me rest, but inside I was rotting for lack of exercise and ministry. I would sometimes cry to my husband and say, "If they would just let me mop the floor."

When we moved back to the States I thought, "Now I can be active once again. I can speak English instead of Japanese, so I will be freer in ministry. I can volunteer for different activities. There are so many things I can do." God seemed to have another plan. Every door I would try to enter would slam shut in my face. I volunteered to help substitute in children's work, but I wasn't called. I volunteered to keep youth in my home for the youth conference, but my home wasn't needed. There was a time when couples were to get together with other couples, but Phil was away. If we went together to minister at a church, the pastor or his wife would say as we were leaving, "Oh, we wish you were here to minister at the ladies' meeting tomorrow." What made it all worse was the fact that my prayers didn't seem to go past the ceiling, even though I faithfully had my devotions each day.

One day I distinctly remember standing in our kitchen in Portland and saying, "God, I'm getting old. This trial has been going on for several years, and you need to answer me now!" Strangely, God didn't seem to do anything. He didn't seem to be at all concerned that I was the ripe old age of fifty-five!

God has His time for everything. My ministry was to me like Isaac was to Abraham. God wanted me to give it to Him. This happened at a New Year's Eve watch night service when I finally said, "OK, God. I am dead. I don't have a ministry, unless you give it to me." Immediately I realized that I had surrendered my all to Him. I had died to what I thought was the ministry He had given to me. I knew that His resurrection in my life had begun. All of this trial was only God's way of opening me up to a greater ministry than I had ever enjoyed previously. As Phil and I talked and prayed, we made some needed changes so we could both feel fulfilled in the ministries God had given us.

In 1999 Pastor Danny Bonilla from New York was preaching in Bible Temple. As he stood at the pulpit, he looked out over the congregation and asked Phil to stand up. He then began prophesying to him that he would go to the nations, over and over again. Sitting next to Phil, I knew that the prophecy was for me too, for we ministered together, but secretly in my heart I was thinking, "It surely would have been nice if I, too, had been prophesied over personally." Later I fully realized why that prophecy was only to Phil. In fact, I was even thankful that it wasn't addressed personally to me!

While Pastor Bonilla was still in Portland, he gave another word to Phil saying, "You will be like Caleb."

Chapter 40

What Did 'Like Caleb' Mean?

—Helen—

Later that year Phil made a trip to Thailand. Wayne and Carolyn Crooke were celebrating the dedication of the church they had built, and they had invited several ministers to the dedication. Phil not only ministered there, but he was at several other places as well. During the trip he had experienced good liberty, strength and anointing. However, when I picked him up, I noticed that he could hardly get up a slight incline while walking through the airport. When we got home and he tried to take a shower, he was exceedingly weak. An electrocardiogram revealed the need for surgery.

Before the operation, the doctor told Phil that his heart was hooked up wrong, but they would correct it during surgery. Something that was supposed to go to his heart was hooked up to his lungs, and he had been living that way for over sixty years!

After the quadruple bypass surgery was over, Phil started having non-stop hiccoughs for over seventeen straight hours. Eventually, he was able to fall asleep in a chair. Since the nurse was hesitant to move him after his long ordeal with hiccoughs, he stayed in the chair all night long. This resulted in a bed sore which took a year to heal.

L to R Rachel, Amber & Autumn (2 of Rachel's children), Sarah, Jon

156 • *Adventures in Faith*

A day or two after surgery, something very significant took place. I opened my Bible to Psalms and read Psalm 27. The whole chapter seemed to be promises concerning Phil, so I testified about it to everyone who came to visit Phil in the hospital that day. That evening our daughter Sarah came and stood beside his bed saying, "Dad, when someone goes through a trial or has surgery, I ask God for a promise for them. I would like to read to you what He gave me for you." I was all ears when she said, "It is found in Psalm 27:2. *'When the wicked came against me to eat up my flesh, My enemies and foes, They stumbled and fell.'*"

Phil needed a lot of care after surgery, so I was with him for about three months. At the end of this time, it was decided that I should go see about the church in Miyoshi, Japan. I had only been gone about a week when one of our daughters phoned me, saying Phil was in the hospital, and the doctor didn't even know if Phil would live through the night. Immediately I began remembering the prophecies over Phil several months previously about being like Caleb, and going to the nations over and over again. Phil was only in his seventies, not eighty-five like Caleb, and he still needed to go to many nations. Then and there I began praying and surrendering Phil to God and to His will, but I also quoted those prophecies to God. They were a great comfort to me and a rock to stand on in time of need.

When I arrived back in Portland, Phil's leg was so swollen that it looked like it could burst. The doctors were still waiting for tests to come back so they would know what the cause was and how to treat it. When the report was back, the doctor told me the name of the problem, but I didn't understand it. I asked, "What is that?" The doctor replied, "It's eating up his flesh." Immediately I remembered that day in the hospital when God had given me Psalm 27 for Phil, and Sarah had specifically read Psalm 27:2 to him. That scripture says, "*When the wicked came against me to eat up my flesh, My enemies and foes, They stumbled and fell.*" God had given us that promise three months earlier!

I found out that Sarah had called Phil to see how he was while I was away. He had felt like maybe he had the flu; but since he hadn't thought it was bad, he had told Sarah he was fine. Thankfully, she had decided to go check on him. Upon arriving at the house, she had put Phil in the car and Rachel had taken him straight to the doctor. He had been too weak to even get into the doctor's office without help, and the doctor had sent him straight to the hospital. Our daughters and others were with him until I arrived.

Now I understood why the Lord had given the prophetic words through Danny Bonilla to Phil and not to me, for it was Phil who was going to go through the trial. I was so thankful I hadn't received a personal prophetic word! It took some months before Phil's leg healed and we were able to travel again.

Chapter 41

Meeting Pastor Onesimus
—Philip—

In 1979 God told me to go to India to be with Ray Jennings in one of his crusades. God also told me that while I was there I would meet a pastor named Onesimus, and that I was supposed to pray for him and help him financially. I obeyed and went to India. The crusade was being held in a place called Adilabad in the State of Andhra Pradesh. The crusade happened to be smaller than usual; but just as God had shown me ahead of time, an Indian pastor came up to me and said, "I am Pastor Onesimus."

Kozumi Kun and Joel Onesimus with his father and mother.

As it turned out, Pastor Onesimus and his wife had three boys and four girls, but they barely had enough to eat. In fact, while I was still in India, one of his daughters died and I attended her funeral.

Pastor Onesimus was pastoring in a Communist village called Govindaraopet where there were about 10,000 people. Outlaws called Naxalites lived in the surrounding forest area, and they would often cause trouble. Even though Pastor Onesimus had no form of transportation, in spite of the dangers he would walk to many of the surrounding villages to minister and share the good news of the gospel.

Helen and I, along with the church in Miyoshi, began supporting that work financially, and we started going to India once a year,

sometimes even more often. We would rent an inter-city taxi and go down the very narrow road to Govindaraopet. One time we had to go across a little stream on the way, and the taxi got stuck in the middle. There was no such thing as a tow truck to pull us out, so we desperately tried again and again to move the car, but nothing happened. Finally, sixteen men arrived and graciously lifted up the whole car and set it on solid ground. Then we were safely on our way again.

—Helen Interrupts—

On one trip to Govindaraopet, I had made several trips by myself to the outdoor toilet behind the house, but one time later, as one of the pastor's daughters was accompanying me, she pointed to a mound of trash that was right by the path and said, "We've not yet been able to kill the king cobra that lives there!" Immediately, I gave thanks in my heart to God for how He had been protecting me.

—Phil Continues—

During this time we came in contact with Pastor Onesimus' son Joel, who had begun pastoring a work in the city. Joel was hungry to hear more about God's plan for His church. The more he heard, the more he wanted to hear. On our first trip to India many years ago, we had worked with the Indian Pentecostal Church. Pastor Onesimus was one of the early pastors in the IPC, as it was called. Joel was working with that group, too, but the IPC had become very legalistic. After hearing God's Word for a time, Joel said, "I want to leave the Indian Pentecostal Church, and have a New Testament Church." His father decided to leave, too.

During many of our earlier trips we had been ministering a lot with a group called New Life Fellowship, and this took us to many places in India. We were blessed in our times of fellowship with them, and we still have fellowship with them. However, as the years passed we began to feel like we should concentrate our efforts more with Joel and his father. It has been wonderful to see how this has been fruitful. We've watched many of the legalistic ways

Mark Anderson & Aby Carbajal in front row at Pastor's Conference

vanish, and the group that began with just two pastors has now become a fellowship of more than four hundred churches under the leadership of Joel and Blessy Onesimus.

Each church is governed by its own local church government, instead of being a denomination or organization, and they are known as Churches Together Fellowship. We try to have a conference for the pastors often and sometimes we have a ladies conference for all of the ladies in the area.

"For we walk by faith, not by sight"—2 Cor. 5:7 • **161**

We are blessed to see many ministries coming out of the fellowship. A number of years ago we were able to begin a small medical ministry. Through the years it has developed, but we are still believing the Lord for a permanent building, for the hospital has had to be moved about six times.

A nursing school was begun by Joel about four years ago at the request of the government. Each year the enrollment has increased, for the school has become one of the best in the area. As of two years ago, there

Nurses training

were one hundred and fifty students, most of whom were Dalits. Every morning the students have the opportunity to attend a time of singing, worship, and Bible teaching before class, if they so desire.

Left: Nurses who were helping in the medical clinic. Right: Mother bathing child on the street.

From time to time, as God supplies, a free medical clinic is held in one of the various slum areas. The living conditions are really bad in these places. The people have no money for medical care, even though, compared to western standards, the care is very cheap. India has no medical plans that can be bought.

Some of the prostitutes children (or other needy children) being cared for by Joel and Blessy

A few years ago the ministry to the prostitutes was begun after Joel learned that his area had one of the highest numbers of prostitutes in Andhra Pradesh. The number of people with AIDS was unusually large, too.

Every two years there has been a meeting called "Youth Quake" where five or six hundred youths gather for four days of refreshing. The services begin with ministry to those who might still be unbe-

lievers; then we minister on the Baptism of the Holy Spirit. I really claim the gift of faith to be in operation so that the young people are easily filled. We like to pray for them during

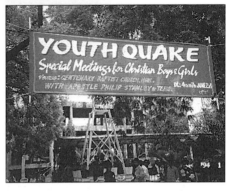

two of the services so that as many as possible have an opportunity to receive.

Most of the Christians in India are Dalits; they are classed in society as the lowest of the low—below the lowest caste. Even though the caste system was supposedly outlawed many years ago, it is very much alive. Since Dalits are usually very poor, the attendees often can't pay for their bus or train fare. Usually the youths are only required to pay about twenty-five cents to attend the conference, but God has been faithful to supply us with what is needed each time as we have stepped forward in faith.

We've had prophetic conferences where two or more prophets have given personal prophetic words to the people. We've also had teaching sessions to help train more natives in prophetic ministry.

Chapter 42

Mexico, Here We Come!

—Helen—

For some years after we went to Japan, I was really homesick for Mexico. We had learned to love the Spanish-speaking people in our early days of ministry, but it seemed as though God had shut the door to those nations all the time we were living in Japan. We had only had the privilege of crossing the border into Mexico one time for a few hours during the whole twenty years of our time

in Japan. However, the Lord began to open the door after we moved back to the States. It was a pretty big adjustment for me to go back to a country where the people hug and kiss each other, after being in Japan where you would never even

Upper Left: Iguala meeting.
Left: Phil, Pastor Lino and Richard Henderson.
Above: Jairo Carbajal and Phil

"For we walk by faith, not by sight"—2 Cor. 5:7 • **165**

touch the other person—you would only bow. During one of those early trips back to Mexico, I can still recall seeing this bearded man who was approaching me to give me a loving, godly kiss. I felt like shrinking into myself or running away. Little by little I got used to it, so that when we went to France and saw that they greeted people with not one but THREE kisses on the cheek, I was able to fit in all right.

Ever since the Lord re-opened Mexico to us, we have been going in and out of it often. We've made many dear friends in many parts of the country. There have been tests, trials and blessings all the way, but the blessings have far outweighed the trials, and the Lord has proved Himself faithful in every way.

Helen: Our Own Home

When we moved to Portland in 1988, we had never owned a home of our own, but I began to desire one. The house we first rented was up for sale, so we went to the bank to see if we could get a loan to buy it. Since we had always paid our bills on time and never borrowed any money, we had no credit. The bank said, "No." Actually, it was God who was saying no, but we didn't understand it at the time.

Phil had said that we might be in Portland for a few years, so my thought was, "If we are going to buy a house, we'd better do it quickly before we leave the country again." I began keeping my eyes open for houses. Phil said he didn't feel like it was quite time yet, but that didn't keep me from looking. One day as I was reading the Bible, my eyes fell on Proverbs 24:27. *"Prepare your outside work, Make it fit for yourself in the field; And afterward build your house."* Then I realized that God's work was more important than a house, so I had a peace. After a time Phil said, "I think we should start looking now."

We didn't look long before we found the house. It was much better than the first house we had wanted, and we had the money to pay for it, even though it was more costly than the first house. We did make payments for a while, because we learned that it would make more financial sense than paying for it outright. But before long we decided to pay off the loan, and we've had plenty of time to enjoy our house. It has been a blessing, too, to have a place where our children, grandchildren and great grandchildren can come, if they so desire. We praise God for His many blessings.

In Closing

To The Regions Beyond
—Helen—

What a joy it has been these twenty-five plus years since we left Japan. We've been able to return to Japan, India and Mexico almost every year. In between those places we've gone to countries like the...

Philippines...

Philip and Bobby Martz

Burma...

Shwedagon temples and the "Burma Road"

"For we walk by faith, not by sight"—2 Cor. 5:7

Thailand...

A service in Thailand

the Ivory Coast...

A church service in the Ivory Coast. Children's service on the street.

European countries, and others as well...

Sometimes the traffic and methods of our transportation have been interesting...

and the various ways of eating have been fun!

We usually stay about a month in each country, and often we go there a number of times. It doesn't matter if it's to a village, town or city; we love all the people whether they live in good or bad conditions or whether there are many or few of them. Occasionally someone asks us, "Which is your favorite country?" We have no answer, for we love them all. Just being in God's will makes each place beautiful!

As we travel, we sometimes hear testimonies from people who have been saved, healed, filled with the Holy Spirit, or just blessed by the messages that we've shared over the years. These testimonies show us that God is at work, even though we don't always know it at the time. As the chorus says, "My Lord knows the way through the wilderness; all I have to do is to follow." God is faithful!

Yoked Together in Christ for 62 Years and On...

170 • *Adventures in Faith*

Made in the USA
Monee, IL
13 May 2021